STEAMING INTO THE BROAD GAUGE

Tales of the Great Western's Daring Experiment

Michael Clutterbuck

HEDDON PUBLISHING

First edition published in 2020 by Heddon Publishing.

Copyright © Michael Clutterbuck 2020, all rights reserved.
No part of this book may be reproduced, adapted, stored in a retrieval system or transmitted by any means, electronic, photocopying, or otherwise without prior permission of the author.

ISBN 978-1-913166-34-2

Cover design by Heddon Publishing.

Cover image courtesy of the Great Western Trust, with thanks to Lawrence Waters.

Map artwork by Catherine Clarke Design.

This is a work of fiction. Names, characters, businesses, places, events and incidents are either the products of the author's imagination or used in a fictitious manner. Any resemblance to actual persons, living or dead, or actual events is purely coincidental.

www.heddonpublishing.com
www.facebook.com/heddonpublishing
@PublishHeddon

This series is dedicated to my late father, William Harold Clutterbuck, himself a railwayman. In giving his son a Hornby train in 1937, he passed on a bug which still claims me firmly. My only regret is that he is no longer with us to see the results. Thank you Dad, for all you did for us.

Introduction

I had long been disappointed in the dearth of British railway fiction and wrote a couple of stories to entertain myself. I passed some of these round to the model railway fraternity here in Melbourne, where they received moderate praise except for from one man, Dr John Ritter. John liked them and urged me to contact a publisher. I did so but after twenty publishers had said they only wanted memoirs or photographs, I gave up. However, one publisher suggested I contact a small local company; they might be interested. I tried again and contacted Katharine Smith at Heddon Publishing, and straightaway hit the jackpot. Initially, I decided that as pensioners we couldn't afford to take a risk financially.

My wife said, "You've been at those stories for ages; go ahead and get them out of your system!"

Now, I usually do what my wife says (I'm not fond of arsenic in my food) so I agreed.

On a trip to the UK in September 2012, my wife, my sister and I were sitting with two young children in the toy-strewn front room of a pleasant terraced house in Shropshire. Kath entered, holding a laptop. "Press that key, Mike," she told me, pointing to the keyboard. I did so, and my first book, the first of the Heddon Publishing titles, was launched.

The following eight years have been, speaking for myself at least, highly rewarding. Dr John Ritter has carefully vetted all the books for technical details, and Geof Sheppard of the Broad Gauge Society has very kindly checked this book for details of the broad gauge period of the Great Western Railway. Kath has guided me through all previous five other books in the *Steaming Into* series.

I cannot express my gratitude well enough to Christa for her acceptance of a husband so often on the keyboard, to John and Geof for their advice, and indeed to Kath for her constant editorial encouragement and support.

Mike Clutterbuck
Melbourne 2020

The Great Western Railway's broad gauge

When the first railways were proposed as Acts of Parliament in the early 1830s, most of them specified a gauge between the rails of four foot, eight-and-a-half inches. This became accepted as a norm. However, I.K. Brunel (one of the country's most widely respected civil engineers and the chosen engineer of the Great Western Railway) chose a much wider gauge of seven feet for his London to Bristol railway. His argument was that he could foresee that railways would become the supreme methods of transportation and would need to carry much larger loads than the 4' 8" would permit. In his application for an Act of Parliament, he carefully omitted to mention his proposed gauge, so that when the Act was passed he was able to persuade his shareholders to accept his much wider specification. Although his engine designs were poor, his young mechanical engineer, Daniel Gooch, was soon able to produce far superior designs, and Brunel's track and gauge structure provided very smooth running. Consequently, the GWR, formed in 1835, was by the later 1840s very successful.

Problems occurred, of course, where other companies met the broader gauge and there was a Parliamentary Commission set up to decide which should be the common gauge of railways in Britain. The only widespread use of the broad gauge was between London and Cornwall, and London and Wolverhampton; the rest of the country's railways both north and south of these routes were almost invariably laid to Stephenson's gauge of 4' 8½".

The commission found that although Brunel's broad gauge had certain advantages, the cost of converting the rest of the country to it would far outstrip any benefit it might bring. The GWR continued building its broad gauge on some of its routes but the problems of transferring goods across GWR territory became so inconvenient that the company was forced to lay a third, narrow gauge rail along many of its routes, to allow narrow gauge trains to run through. By the 1860s, the company began to abandon its broad gauge and convert its routes to the now standard gauge. It maintained, however, its premier line to the West until May 1892, when, over one incredible weekend, the whole route from Paddington to Penzance was narrowed and the broad gauge was dead.

In hindsight, some modern engineers believe that Brunel may have been right and our railways had lost a golden opportunity. Even today, many railways have a wider gauge than the international standard: Ireland, Australia, Russia, Spain, India, Brazil and Argentina are just a few. In the 1940s, Hitler's engineers even planned a vast network across Europe with a gauge of three metres, big enough for frigate hulls built in north German shipyards to be transported by train to the Black Sea, thus avoiding the attention of the Royal Navy!

Great Western and associated companies' main lines 1868

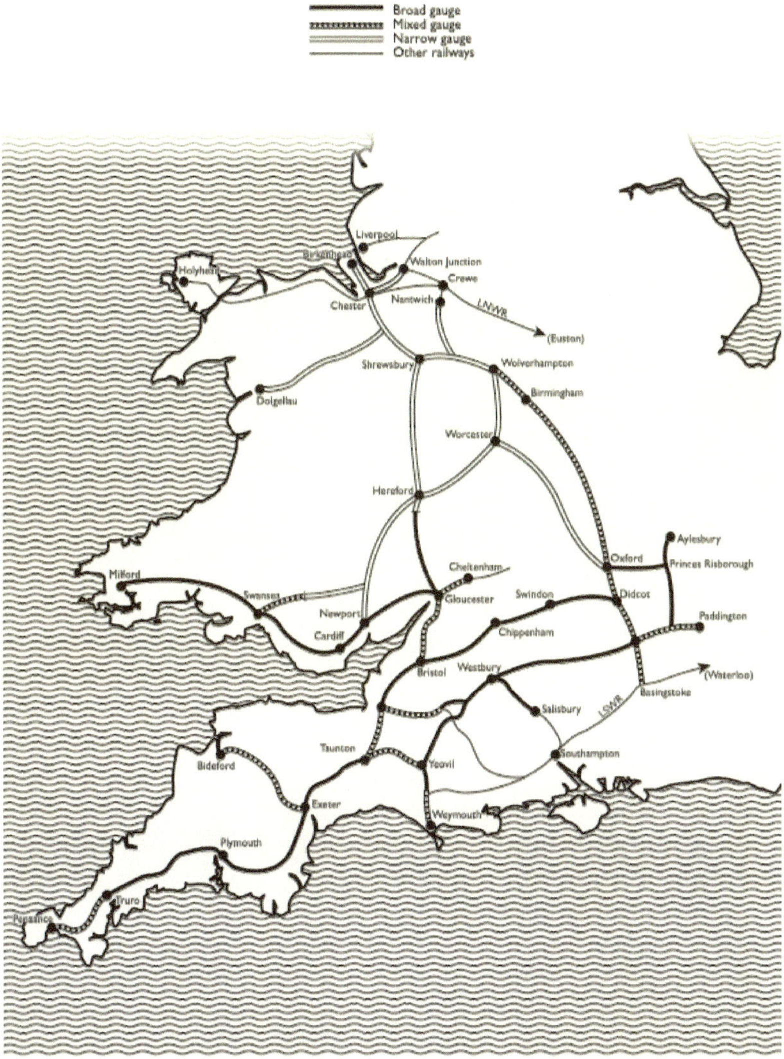

- Broad gauge
- Mixed gauge
- Narrow gauge
- Other railways

Steaming into the Broad Gauge
Tales of the Great Western's Daring Experiment

1 - Henry Denton finds his niche (1848 - 1862) 1
2 - Henry moves south (October 1863) 7
3 - Henry meets the broad gauge (August 1864) 13
4 - Problems at Salop (June 1865) 20
5 - Problems in Gloucester (February 1867) 26
6 - Life in a running shed (July 1868) 32
7 - Under London on the broad gauge (September 1868) ... 38
8 - Pride comes before a fall (April 1869) 44
9 - A Cornish complication (November 1871) 50
10 - Transfer to Chippenham (May 1872) 56
11 - The bullion train (1873) 62
12 - The Slough Slip (1873) 68
13 - A ride on the 'Narrow' again (March 1879) 74
14 - "Good job it were broad gauge!" (September 1881) ... 81
15 - An affair of the heart (1882) 87
16 - Lord Willoughby's journey (March 1888) 94
17 - Driver Denton meets an Iron Duke (November 1891) .101
18 - Driver Denton's broad gauge finale (April 1892) 108
19 - Henry's conquest at Wellington (November 1903) 114
20 - A Star is born (September 1907) 120
Technical vocabulary 126

1 - Henry Denton finds his niche
(1848 - 1862)

At three o'clock in the morning, it was cold in the little Cheshire farm kitchen. That said, there was a faint suggestion of heat still in the ashes of the fire, next to the kitchen range upon which a kettle was already boiling. The girl was busy setting out clean cloths as the farmer paced impatiently to and fro, glancing occasionally out of the window and watching for the appearance of the lamps on the doctor's pony and trap. The lad had been sent out to the village of Tarvin and had returned with the news that Doctor Morgan would be on his way within the hour.

But the farmer must not have been paying attention, because the door burst open and the burly doctor stalked in. "Right ho, Joseph, where is she?"

"Ah, Doctor, thank the good lord you're here. She's been in labour for several hours. She's lying on the settle in the back room."

"Then I'll go in and see what's to be done. You stay here, but I'll need your Gertie with me. Come along, Gertie, this'll need a woman's assistance." The girl and the doctor disappeared into the next room, from where periodic cries and encouraging mutterings could be heard. Joseph tried to sit and relax but couldn't, in spite of Gertie popping her head in frequently to say that all was well.

All at once, there was a load groan, then the sound of a smack, followed by a shrill cry. The new arrival was expressing his indignation at being hauled out of his warm and comforting surroundings and into a cold environment, followed by a brutal attack on his tiny bottom. The crying was, however, rapidly silenced as he was cuddled and wrapped, and his mouth carefully placed where it found a soothing drink.

Master Henry George Denton had arrived in the world.

Joseph and Annie Denton's boy followed the expected path of a farmer's son and grew accustomed to the early milking, feeding the chickens, and chivvying the cattle around when they were transferred to a new field.

Young Henry found the work mainly to his liking and didn't think about doing anything different as he grew older. But all this changed one early winter's day, when his family visited an elderly aunt who lived in the county capital of Chester. Before their return to the farm, they spent a little time in the city so that Henry's mother could do some shopping. Joseph decided, like a good many husbands, that shopping was not for him, so he took his son into the Pied Bull, a Chester coaching inn, where a coach and four for London had just pulled in. The ostlers were unhitching the tired horses and the fresh ones were being brought out.

"Hurry up you men, I have to be in London by Wednesday night!" came an angry shout from inside the coach.

"An' you will be, sir, barrin' 'ighwaymen. This 'ere coach will 'ave you there in two days, sir. Allus does." The comforting words of the ostler rang out across the yard.

Inside the inn, two of the customers at the bar were apparently unhappy with certain aspects of modern life. Joseph ordered himself a pint and a glass of small beer for his son, and they sat near the two worthies.

"No good'll come of 'em, let me tell yer," said one crusty old gent to his even more ancient neighbour.

"Yer doan't need ter convince me, Jacob," replied the other.

Henry's father leaned over. "No good'll come of what?" he enquired.

"Why, these new railaways. We've even got 'em 'ere now. Yer can get ter Birken'ead in an hour, an' ter Wrexham an' all."

"But," added his neighbour, "I'll tell yer wot they can't do. If you want ter get ter Wrexham, they can't be sure ter get yersel' there; why, it were only a coupla years back they dropped one o' them trains in the River Dee."

"Aye, so they did." The first gent supported his neighbour's point. "A niece o' mine were in that train too. She weren't killed like the five others, but she were three months in 'orspital, an' when she came out she were nivver right in the 'ead agen."

"Yes, I see that, but surely getting to London in ten hours is an improvement on two days?"

"Can't see it meself. Why is ever'one in such a' urry these days?"

Later, when they drove the trap past the railway station, young Henry could hardly contain his excitement. He had heard of trains, of course, but had never actually seen one. The engines with their long funnels and big domed fireboxes reminded him of steam kettles (which, in a sense, they were); the railway coaches he thought very like stagecoaches, but they could carry dozens of people at a continuing speed that no stagecoach could maintain on the rough roads. He knew, too, that you could even get to far distant London within a day; a journey unthinkable even by modern stagecoach standards.

Joseph's father noted the boy's increasing enthusiasm with dismay; his young son was showing more interest in the railway than a farmer's boy ought. Even now, he could sense that he might lose the boy from the farm if this passion were to be encouraged. He determined to try and distract his lad by giving him more responsibility. This tactic worked for a short time but by the time his son reached the age of twelve, Joseph had to admit defeat. Young Henry was never going to be a farmer. He had his eyes firmly set on joining the railway service.

Two years later, Henry had already been employed for twelve months at Saltney Works, in a suburb of Chester. This was the headquarters of the small Shrewsbury & Chester Railway, which had been bought out by the huge Great Western Railway a few years earlier. Henry was by this time familiar with many of the duties around the works and had even been on some of the engines as they moved about the sidings. He knew to break up the lumps of coal to make it easier for the fireman to shovel them into the firebox. He had been employed as a firelighter on several occasions, starting with a small box of wood chips and shavings in the firebox before covering it with small lumps of coal once it had begun to burn. He knew to visit the fire regularly to build it up to the stage where it could heat the boiler enough to boil off steam at a pressure that met the driver's satisfaction and allowed the engine to move. He also knew of the danger of building up the pressure too far and causing an explosion. The engines had safety valves that were meant to prevent this, but sometimes drivers tampered with them to increase the pressure, thus allowing them to move a train which was really too heavy for the locomotive.

By 1862, boiler explosions were rare; locomotive builders' knowledge of metallurgy and design had improved, and most drivers and fitters had learned the folly of tampering with the safety valves. Nevertheless, explosions were still possible and the travelling public were understandably unhappy if accidents occurred, their unhappiness reflecting in company takings. The 'railway mania' of the 1840s had bankrupted many investors, although the railway industry was still a fiercely competitive business, with fights in boardrooms. Even vigorous fisticuffs between competing company employees in joint stations were by no means unknown. Indeed, Chester itself had been the scene of a fierce battle between employees of the London & North Western Railway, and those of the Shrewsbury & Chester Railway a dozen years earlier.

Although young Denton was used on a wide range of duties, such as assisting the carpenters on wagon repairs, loading and unloading the wagons and vans, fetching and carrying for the tally clerks, it was the engines themselves that caught his imagination. He loved working with the enginemen and his day was made on the rare occasions that he rode on the footplate up and down the yard. If he could do something for a driver, he was quite prepared to spend an extra couple of hours, especially if this meant he could mount the cab and watch the driver at his controls, or even pull some of the coal forward on the tender for the fireman.

Riding the older engines around the yard was a particular delight and Henry soon learned how to grab onto the single handrail (if the engine had one) while it lurched its way forwards or in reverse.

One morning, he was asked by a fireman to actually sustain the fire while the latter fetched his lunch. The returning fireman watched with approval and showed Henry that simply shovelling coal straight into the firebox was not enough; you had to twist the shovel to get the coal where it was most needed. This was a skill that needed experience and practice.

As the months passed, Henry found himself more often used as an assistant fireman, and got used to firing for short spells in the yard. One never-to-be-forgotten afternoon, he was told to accompany a fireman on a short goods to Chester. The works foreman had noticed Henry's interest and obvious ability, and decided to give him a chance to show what he could be capable of. There was little formal training for footplate work and railway officials were always looking for men who showed inherent nous. Driver Jed Rowsley had agreed to Henry's presence on his engine, provided that his regular fireman was there to keep an eye on the young lad as he handled the shovel for the first time.

The run from Saltney Yard to Chester Station was only a two-mile stretch, mostly over the important Chester & Holyhead Railway's tracks, but it gave both men an opportunity to see how their young charge could manage on a main line. The short train would not unduly tax a regular fireman, but it could give valuable experience to a budding engineman.

Forwarding goods trains from the south to Birkenhead had previously been a contentious issue as the Chester and

Birkenhead Railway had been heavily under the influence of Captain Huish, general manager of the powerful London and North Western Railway, who had tried hard to prevent his great rival the Great Western from reaching the Mersey. But his often illegal shenanigans had backfired badly: he had driven the Shrewsbury & Chester and the Shrewsbury & Birmingham railways into the very hands of the GWR, thus thwarting his own ambitious plan.

The only problem for the GWR was that they couldn't continue their broad gauge system beyond Wolverhampton, as the two Shrewsbury railways had never contemplated widening their track gauge out to seven feet, and in any case would not have had the necessary funds to allow this.

Once in Chester, the short train was duly passed over to the Birkenhead Railway, and the two Saltney enginemen were well pleased with the efforts and achievement of their young companion, promising him that they would give him a good report, always assuming his return trip was equally acceptable. It was, and as a result Henry was allowed to fire short trips under the watchful eye of a regular fireman. He frequently fired to Chester, and later to Rossett and Wrexham, on a range of locomotives but always on short goods trains.

On one magical occasion, he was allowed on a large passenger engine, taking a train to Wrexham and back. This was a heavy train and Henry spent most of the time on the large tender, shovelling coal forward so that the fireman, who had hurt his hand that morning, could stay working and earn his pay.

In his digs that evening, he wrote his father an apologetic letter, regretting that he could not see himself taking over the farm. Instead, he would be an engineman and work for the mighty Great Western Railway.

2 - Henry moves south
(October 1863)

It had been raining heavily and there was little in the way of shelter at Saltney, but Henry was used to working out in all weathers, from his boyhood assisting his father on the farm. He was carrying a heavy bag of tools to the engineer working on one of the 0-6-0 long-boilered goods engines. The engine had been involved in a minor accident and needed some attention to the right-hand footplate, where damage had been done to the handrail on the driver's side.

"Any problem with this job, Mr Dickson?" asked Henry.

Jack Dickson looked up with a smile as he saw Henry approaching "Not really, young Denton," he replied. "A few careful thumps with the hammer should straighten the handrail and make the crew feel a bit safer. Mind you," he added, "the blokes don't like these engines much."

"Why's that, then? Are they too old?" Henry knew that these engines were almost twenty years old.

"No, it's not that. They have a very short wheelbase, which makes them unsteady. That's not such a problem for the goods engines but with the passenger engines it can be dangerous. It was one of them that came off the road last year and killed its driver and a dozen passengers."

Before Henry could pursue the matter further, another driver came over and called out to him "Hey, Denton, the foreman wants you in his office now so cut along quick as you can."

In the office, the foreman stared at him for a moment or two, then said, "I'm going to do you a favour, young Denton."

"Sir?"

"You're still young; what it is? Fifteen?"

"Yessir."

"Shrewsbury is looking for another cleaner and I have suggested you. You might still be a nipper but you learn quickly and you're enthusiastic. There's talk of closing these railway works down so you might be out of a job later if you stay here."

"Thank you, sir."

"I've had a word with my colleague in Shrewsbury, who's been looking for a useful young fellow to learn to work in railway service, and I've told him that you might be worth considering. You start there next week and see if you like it there. I am giving you a day off to go and find yourself somewhere to live in Shrewsbury. Good luck!"

Three weeks later, in Coleham Shed in Shrewsbury, Henry felt himself to be in a completely different world; the GWR shed was adjacent to the LNWR shed and both were far larger than the Saltney Works he was used to. He soon began to travel in new directions, 'learning the road', as it was called.

He was already familiar with the road north to Wrexham and Chester, having travelled it on occasions, assisting fitters with recalcitrant locomotives that had caused problems along the route.

The shedmaster at the big shed at Coleham was a short, no-nonsense man who gave Henry no more than a passing glance from his desk then proceeded to address him whilst flicking through some paperwork.

"You start here as a cleaner at a shilling a week, with some firing duties as soon as I can be sure that what your Saltney foreman told me was true. If you're as good as he claims, you'll be firing within a short time. We need another fireman or two for emergencies."

"Thank you, sir."

"Have you found digs here?"

"Yessir, in Moreton Crescent."

"Very convenient, I must say; you are fortunate."

"Sir."

"Well, report immediately to Chargehand Simmonds; he looks after the cleaning gangs. I'll check with him as to your progress in three months."

"Sir."

Henry left the office determined to see that his progress

in the next three months would be sufficient to elevate him to firing duties.

The work as a cleaner at the Coleham Shed was rather more demanding than he'd been used to as a lowly odd-job man at Saltney, but he enjoyed the tighter discipline that Chargehand Simmonds enforced. Cyril Simmonds knew what he wanted and how to get it from his cleaners; he was firm but fair and was generally respected by the cleaning gangs, but all cleaners were well aware of what to expect if they crossed the line. It didn't happen very often but when it did the results were dramatic enough to discourage repeats of whatever the offence may have been.

For Henry Denton, the time he spent learning the job was a rewarding experience that made him thankful to have chosen to work on the railway rather than staying on the family farm. One particular job he undertook was that of bar-boy. This meant climbing into the firebox to clean the firebars and checking the firebricks. They had to be cleared of clinker and ash so that the air from the ash pan was not hampered in bringing oxygen to the fire to encourage steaming. He would also have to ensure that any loose firebricks in the brick arch were replaced.

One morning, he was told to assist with a fitter in replacing the coupling rods on an older express 2-4-0 ex-Shrewsbury & Chester engine. He learned how the rods were fixed on the axles and the difficulties of greasing to maintain a constant flow of grease during the run, easing friction between the journals of the rods and their axles. A really satisfactory method had not been developed by any of the railway companies and most were experimenting to find a solution.

Henry also learned that engines with only a short distance between the driving wheel centres gave rough riding.

Coleham Shed in Shrewsbury was unusual in that it was actually two sheds owned by different companies, each maintaining its stud of engines alongside the competition.

The London & North Western and the Great Western railways jointly owned the route from Shrewsbury to Hereford and here, curiously, they seemed to be able to get along amicably, whereas elsewhere they sometimes fought tooth and nail. Both sets of employees worked separately in their respective workplaces but met on occasions over their sandwiches and discussed the relative merits of their companies' locomotives, often indulging in some friendly banter. The names of their chief engineers, Webb of the LNWR and Gooch of the GWR, were bandied about, especially among the younger workers, as if they actually knew the great men.

The Great Western used the route for its trains from Bristol or South Wales to the docks at Saltney or Birkenhead, or from the coal mines of Gresford in both directions, and its passenger trains from Chester and Birkenhead to Bristol and South Wales. The LNWR ran their trains from Manchester or Liverpool, via Crewe, to Hereford and South Wales. Consequently, locomotives of both companies shared the haulage on the Shrewsbury to Hereford run. One result of this was that Henry occasionally found himself in the cab of a North Western engine running from the shed to the station or vice versa: all very unofficially, of course.

In Salop (as Shrewsbury was generally known by the rail fraternity) as in Saltney, Henry's enthusiasm and ability soon got him noticed by senior management. His eagerness to volunteer for all aspects of railway work – a feature of his personality he would later to pass on to his son with very positive results – brought him a rapid promotion to local firing duties. His only problem was that he had earned the strong dislike of Alec Clarkson's cleaning gang.

"Hey Denton, you're spendin' too much time on that safety valve! This is a goods engine; it's not goin' to haul 'er Majesty!"

"I just want it to be clean."

"In my gang, I decide whether it's clean, not you. You're takin' too long on a simple job."

"But I—"

"Don't argue with me, boy. You might do some firin' sometimes but you're on my gang an' you'll do what I tell you."

Cleaner Clarkson was a lazy man and did not insist on his gang achieving a spotless locomotive. He had always scoffed at Henry's rather more stringent insistence that any engine he worked on had to be sent out in pristine condition.

Henry learned the routes to Craven Arms, Wellington, Welshpool and Kidderminster, and assisted in the firing on some of the heavier trains. He was hoping for an official promotion to firing duties and he was unofficially allotted to Driver Huw Pryce whenever Driver Pryce's regular fireman was unavailable. 'Prycey' was popular among his colleagues. He was easy-going, which meant that he was not prone to be unduly critical of Henry's occasional errors. On the other hand, he did not give Henry the advice that might have been expected from him, and Henry had to learn much by his own observation.

The other problem Henry had was that he was much further away from his family, which saddened both him and his parents. His wages were too small to be able to travel home very often. Consequently, he gave full attention to his work in the shed. He found it enjoyable and made strenuous efforts to improve, but again this did not go down well with some of his colleagues, and not just Alex Clarkson's gang. Even some of the senior drivers took umbrage when he commented on the appearance of their engines.

One of them said angrily to him one morning, "If Alec Clarkson the senior cleaner is satisfied, who're you to criticise, you cheeky young pup?"

"But when the engines are clean, the trains look so much better," argued Henry. "It makes people want to travel on our trains."

"Passengers use our trains because they want to travel somewhere; it don't matter what the engines look like!" countered the driver.

"But—" began Henry.

"But nothing!" snarled the driver. "You do what you're

told by your seniors and button your lip. If you ever get to fire on my engine, you'll very soon find out what happens when insolent young sprogs get above their station!"

Over the next two or three months, Henry was given a range of duties by the observant Chargehand Simmonds, who had noticed that the young man was not popular in Clarkson's gang. He took Henry out of the gang occasionally, to try him out on other duties, but this gave the chargehand something of a dilemma. On the one hand, it relieved the internal pressure on Clarkson's gang but on the other, it gave rise to an accusation of favouritism in the shed.

With Henry moving between the cleaning gang and these extra duties, Chargehand Simmonds knew it was not ideal, but for the moment, he could not think of any alternative arrangement. However, he knew that sooner or later he would have to take firm action.

In the meantime, Henry did indeed 'button his lip' when on cleaning duties with the gang, and tried to fit in with their lax habits, although it irked him. The occasions when he was given a different duty were bright intervals in an otherwise frustrating job.

In spite of his disappointment with his co-workers, Henry felt that working and learning on the Great Western Railway was turning out to be a very satisfactory career and much more to his liking than working on the farm.

3 - Henry meets the broad gauge (August 1864)

On one very wet morning in late summer, Henry had an unusual duty. He was waiting on the footplate of a locomotive and wondering what it would be like to have work under cover or, like the passengers, travel inside a comfortable wooden box on wheels with a roof over his head, rather than face the rain or snow while he fired the engine. He had been tasked to fire on a Birmingham goods as far as Wolverhampton: a place which was new to him. This was to see whether he could handle such a duty.

It was raining heavily at Wolverhampton and as the wind was from the north the engine's low spectacle plate gave the crew heading south no protection whatsoever. But, well used to such adverse conditions from having been brought up on a farm, Henry just shrugged his shoulders and got on with his duties.

Approaching Wolverhampton, he was surprised to see the trackwork outside the station; it looked very strange. Some of it appeared to be far too wide for the rolling stock, but his driver ran onto it without any obvious concern.

"What sort of trackwork is this, Mr Pryce?" Henry asked in astonishment.

"Oh, the Great Western broad gauge terminates here," his driver replied.

"Broad gauge?"

"Yes, didn't you know? Most of the Great Western Railway runs on a wider gauge than ours. But it's mainly in the south, and sooner or later they will change it all to our gauge."

"Why did they make it so wide?"

"Ah, that was the work of Mr Brunel, our first engineer. He decided that a seven-foot gauge would be better than that of the Liverpool & Manchester Railway when he started to build our railway. He thought the trains could carry heavier loads and would go faster."

"So why is our railway around Shrewsbury not in the wider gauge?"

"That's because the Shrewsbury railways were built for the gauge used by most railways. Then, when we became part of the Great Western system, it was too expensive to change."

"Are the broad gauge trains faster?"

"Well, I don't know, lad, but the broad gauge men all seem to prefer them."

They pulled into the station and Henry jumped down to detach their coaches from the locomotive, so that they could back up to the shed and service and turn their engine. Having readied it, they ran back to the station and backed onto their return train.

"Look at that, Mr Pryce!" Henry stared eagerly as an enormously wide engine passed them on its way to the shed. It was a – to Henry's eyes – huge 4-2-2, with the name *Lightning* on its side. It was vastly bigger than any locomotive Henry had ever seen. Driver Huw Pryce looked to where the lad was pointing and said, "Ah yes, you don't see many of them broad gauge engines up here these days. Must be a special."

"Have you ever driven one?"

Driver Pryce shook his head. "Can't say I have, lad; but I once fired one. Never again!"

"Why? What's wrong with them?"

"I only fired it a short distance, but that firebox is huge and eats coal faster than you can throw it in!"

"But they're impressive locomotives, don't you think, Mr Pryce?"

"Aye, they do look good, I'll give you that, lad. But they won't last."

"Won't last? Why not?"

"This broad gauge is too much of a nuisance. It makes sending freight and passengers between north and south inconvenient. Everything has to change trains where there's a different gauge. Even the Great Western and the Bristol & Exeter railways know they will have to get rid of it sooner or later."

Clearly, Driver Pryce felt no enthusiasm for the broad gauge. Henry, however, admired the size and majesty of the great engine and wished he could work on one.

This wish came true very quickly when he found himself in the centre of a minor crisis. Wolverhampton was the northern limit of the broad gauge, and although broad gauge trains were by this time rare here, they did occasionally appear.

The broad gauge engine returned to its train on the main up line and as Henry was admiring the locomotive, the driver saw him and invited him onto the footplate. Henry accepted with alacrity. He couldn't believe the amount of space the engine crew had on the footplate of this monster Iron Duke 4-2-2 compared to his 'narrow gauge' (as most GWR men referred to it) engines. The brass fittings on the backhead were gleaming and polished; clearly, this driver was proud of his engine. The enormous shining dome of the firebox inspired belief in the power of the engine. The footplate area, however, was without any real weather protection: there were only handrails on both sides for crewmen to lean on.

"This here's one of them early engines," remarked the driver. "She's got no frills. But I've heard talk of new ones being built with side panels they call side sheets."

"I've been told they can run fast, these engines," said Henry.

"Aye, you've been told right," replied the driver.

"One cove told me that they can do fifty miles an hour," Henry continued.

Driver Morton laughed, "Fifty? We've done eighty in this old kettle, haven't we, Billy?" This latter remark to his fireman up on the tender, pulling coal forward to ease his work later in the journey.

The fireman looked up and smiled. "Aye, we 'ave." He

continued with his shovelling.

"How d'you keep your feet at eighty miles an hour?" asked Henry.

"That's when you have to grab the handrail and hold tight," replied the driver, "but Mr Brunel's track is the best in the country and the run is much smoother than on other railways."

Henry nodded, "Yes, I've heard that. too. So it's true?"

"Billy and I have done the Didcot to Paddington run in an hour, averaging at well over fifty. It can be done with these engines."

"An hour to Paddington?" Henry couldn't believe this "An hour?"

"Certainly, and we've done it more'n once."

Henry was deeply impressed. He determined to get himself transferred to the broad gauge as soon as he could.

Most employees of the Great Western, in spite of the conclusions of the Gauge Commissioners over twenty years earlier, considered that their broad gauge was superior to that of the standard gauge, and that they had been hard done by to be forced to abandon it.

Indeed, even the commissioners themselves had noted that the wider gauge had distinct technical advantages, in that trains could, with their effectively lower centre of gravity, be more stable, carry greater loads, and, with Brunel's fine trackwork, travel at impressive speeds. So, in 1863, most of the GWR in the south still maintained the broad gauge, although an increasing proportion of it was slowly becoming 'dual gauge', through the addition of an extra rail to allow standard gauge trains along the routes.

The fireman on the coal in the tender turned to climb down to the footplate. As he did so, his foot slipped and jammed itself between two big lumps of coal. He tumbled forward into the cab with a yell of pain. Both the driver and Henry hurried to the luckless fireman, to help him back onto his feet but when they got him there he could not stand.

"You're no damn use to me in that condition, Billy," grumbled the driver, staring at his mate. "You'll have to get yourself fixed up and I'll need a spare fireman."

But the shedmaster informed him that there was no spare available and that the nearest place which could provide one was Birmingham.

"My return train to Salop isn't due to leave for an hour and a half," Henry chipped in. "I don't know the road to Birmingham but if the driver will have me, I'll be happy to help out as far as Snow Hill."

"But you're a narrow man," protested the driver "Have you ever fired a broad gauge engine?"

"If I'm honest – no," admitted Henry. "But I could at least keep you moving."

The shedmaster pondered for a few moments then said, "If you wait for a spare fireman, Driver Morton, you could easily be five hours. I am prepared to allow this young fellow to fire to you as far as Snow Hill, if your fireman can keep an eye on him."

"Doesn't seem as if I have much choice, sir. Right, lad," the driver said to Henry, "there's your shovel and there's the firebox!"

Billy, the injured fireman, was given first aid before being helped up back into the cab, where he kept out of Henry's way. Henry grasped the shovel, opened the firebox, and stared inside. He gasped at the size of it. How the devil am I going to fire this enormous cavern?

Driver Morton watched Henry's face and chuckled: "Your mouth, lad, is nearly as big as my firebox! You should learn to keep it shut at important moments! Don't worry, Billy'll show you as we go."

As they paused in the station to couple up to their train, the Wolverhampton shedmaster came along the platform and informed Henry that there was a down goods through Snow Hill for Birkenhead, due about twenty minutes after their arrival there. Henry should be sure to be on time in order to return on it.

Henry fired the huge engine on their run to Birmingham

and found out that the big firebox was not as greedy as expected. It was nevertheless hard to fire because the coal had to be spread evenly across it. But even as he persevered, he noticed how forgiving that firebox was, once he learned to maintain a nice even bed of coal over the whole grate. Then he noticed how smooth the run was, even though the train was travelling faster than he was used to on the 'narrow' gauge lines.

The short run to Snow Hill turned out to be less of a trial than he expected. Apart from the tricky firing, other features of the job were much the same as on the engines he was used to.

Over the next few months, Henry thought hard about his experience on that broad gauge engine. Every time he landed at Wolverhampton or Birmingham, he hoped to see another, but that didn't happen too often. All of the country north of Wolverhampton was standard gauge and much of it south of London was mixed gauge as well. Only the lines in the triangle between London, Penzance and South Wales were mostly broad gauge.

This difference in gauges made rail connections between north and south extremely inconvenient, and the GWR was gradually forced into providing mixed gauge, to allow connections with the LNWR and the Midland railways in the north, and the London & South Western and London Brighton & South Coast to the south. Yet by 1866 there were still twenty breaks of gauge, which of course were a serious hindrance to the travelling public as well as to goods traffic. The only allies of the GWR's broad gauge were the Bristol & Exeter Railway and the smaller broad gauge railway companies in Devon and Cornwall, which worked closely with the GWR to allow through trains from Paddington to Penzance.

In 1865, Daniel Gooch, the previous chief engineer of the company, had become the chairman and had, with great reluctance, accepted the need to abandon the broad gauge. Even as early as 1861, the third rail had reached Paddington itself, allowing standard gauge through trains from Birkenhead to terminate in the capital. Yet most long-distance trains from Paddington to the West Country were still broad gauge, and much appreciated by the passengers for their speed and comfort, only partially matched by the standard gauge railways. Indeed, the main line to the west was to be dominated by broad gauge trains for almost thirty more years.

4 – Problems at Salop (June 1865)

Cleaner Henry Denton was a man uplifted by his experience of firing to a large broad gauge locomotive and he was wondering how he could get to repeat the experience. He had always enjoyed his work on the standard gauge but working on the footplate of a broad gauge engine was, he felt, a very satisfying experience indeed.

His thoughts along such lines were abruptly and unpleasantly interrupted a few days later, in Shrewsbury Shed. The exuberance of his pleasure at firing a 'proper' Great Western engine was salt in the wound of the jealousy of Cleaner Alec Clarkson at Henry's rapid promotion to firing duties ahead of the older man.

The fault, however, was not entirely on Clarkson's side; Henry himself had made little secret of his new feelings of superiority. Most of the men of Salop Shed hailed from standard gauge areas and did not share his enthusiasm for the wider gauge, and Henry's constant lauding of its qualities began to make him unpopular, even among those who appreciated his obvious abilities. As a result, there was often hostility between those few who sided with Henry in their belief in the broad gauge, and the great majority (including, naturally, the men from the neighbouring LNWR shed) who did not. This particularly disturbed Emrys Hughes, the Salop shedmaster. Hitherto, his shed had been a relatively peaceful place; he and his neighbouring LNWR shedmaster colleague had co-operated well to prevent any latent problems between the employees of the two companies. Shedmaster Hughes was therefore annoyed that there should be ill-feeling among his own men. He was a Welshman from Wrexham, on the old Shrewsbury & Chester Railway, which had never shown the slightest interest in the broad gauge, even after amalgamation with the GWR. In any case, the Shrewsbury & Chester had never been in any financial state to consider it.

His problem was exacerbated one evening, after a particularly irate exchange of insults between the two cleaners, egged on by colleagues eager to see fisticuffs ending in blood-letting. The noise brought the angry shedmaster out and he hauled both men into his office.

"I don't damn well care what you two are fighting about, but it will stop here and now. Clarkson and Denton, you are both fined three days' pay!" The shedmaster was determined that their bickering should cease. "And if it happens once more, you'll both be out on your ears."

But two days later, reading a circular from Head Office in Paddington, he could see his problem solved. He called Henry Denton back into his office.

"You are preventing me, Cleaner Denton, from having a quiet and effective workplace," he said. "You are an excellent worker, but you have more pride than is good for you."

Henry Denton paled, feeling he was about to get the sack. "I will try to stay away from Clarkson, sir," he began, but was interrupted by his foreman.

"Oh yes, most certainly. You will be leaving Salop as soon as I can arrange it. It would be a crime for the Great Western to lose a man with your potential, so I am sending you to Paddington, to see if they can find a duty somewhere else for you."

Henry left the shedmaster's office in disappointment. Shrewsbury was already far enough from his family farm near Chester. Paddington might find somewhere even further away.

Henry's trip to London was a mixed blessing: despite his concern at being moved further away from his family, the ride to Paddington was fascinating. His train terminated at Birmingham and he had to change there. The difference between the journey in a standard gauge train and the broad gauge train to Paddington was startling. His previous experience of a broad gauge train was only the few miles or so between Wolverhampton and Birmingham Snow Hill, and that was on the footplate of a locomotive. There was nothing smooth about working on a footplate, regardless of the track gauge. Everything shook and rattled, and a crewman had to learn how to keep on his feet to put the coal into the firebox exactly where it was needed. If anything, it was harder on the broad gauge, as the firebox grate area was so much wider and consequently the coal had to be placed more precisely in order to establish a thin but even fire that would suit the driver's requirements for steam. But on this vast footplate, Henry had noticed the difference. The ride was noticeably more even, especially during those few minutes when he did not have to fire and could relax for a moment or two.

Riding in the carriage, however, was a revelation to him: it was far superior. Of course, he had ridden in carriages on the standard gauge many times when travelling to or from home, and had been used to making smug comparisons between the ride in a train compared to that of a horse and dogcart on roads which were frequently potholed and poorly maintained. But even a railway carriage could sway and jerk, depending on the state of the track; especially on the tracks of a small company like the Shrewsbury & Chester Railway, with its limited finances and maintenance. Its takeover by the huge Great Western organisation had not yet brought about the hoped-for improvements.

But the broad gauge baulk trackwork was beginning to require very expensive maintenance to confer the claimed superior ride as regards speed and comfort. Its designer, I.K. Brunel, had been a brilliant civil engineer, although it had to be admitted that his railway locomotives had not been a success. In fact, young Daniel Gooch, the mechanical engineer Brunel had appointed, swiftly had them rebuilt, or replaced them with his own superior designs.

As he reposed in relaxed comfort, Henry wondered whether the Gauge Commissioners twenty years earlier had actually experienced travel in a broad gauge train when they decided in favour of the standard gauge for Britain's railway systems. The 'narrow' gauge had even penetrated

Paddington and through trains from Birkenhead could now reach the capital without requiring passengers to change at Oxford, thereby reducing the journey time.

Paddington Station was an eye-opener for Henry: it was vast, with its vaulted glazed roof, and entirely broad gauge, with the concession of some mixed gauge tracks. He thought it must be a serious challenge for those who had to design and construct the trackwork, just as for the shunters and linesmen who had to work with it. But his meeting at the Old Oak Common shed turned out to be short-lived.

"No, son," the shedmaster said to him, "I've no need for another cleaner, and I don't understand why the Salop shedmaster sent you here; we don't deal with footplate staffing, that's done at Swindon. You'll have to go there."

This required another trip, this time on the broad gauge, giving Henry a chance once more to appreciate its proficiency. His pleasure was diminished, however, when he realised that the staffing office would be closed by the time he arrived. Not having expected to stay overnight, he was reduced to sleeping in the station waiting room.

At six in the morning, he reported to the main gate at Swindon Works, to be directed to the staffing office. The officer in charge opened Henry's letter from the Shrewsbury shedmaster and read it carefully.

"Hmm. Your shed foreman thinks highly of you, Cleaner Denton. He thinks you will go far. Now, as it happens, I have a request from the shed foreman at Oxford for two enginemen, so I will appoint you as one of them. You will still be a cleaner, but with diligence and hard work you may find yourself driving within ten years. You can start next Monday and you will need to have your possessions sent on to Oxford from Salop."

Henry's work at Oxford was at first a total thrill. He was on the broad gauge at last! Yet when he was first firing the big engines, he was reminded of the vicar's words when, as a boy, he attended a funeral with his family in their Cheshire village: "The Lord giveth, and the Lord taketh away." He had puzzled over these words until his teacher had explained that they were a misquotation from the Book of Job and they meant that nothing was perfect. Nevertheless, it didn't take long to get used to the broad gauge engines, and their own set of peculiarities. Passenger trains to the north, to Birmingham, were still broad gauge, so he was now rarely on standard gauge locomotives, although through trains from Paddington to Chester or Birkenhead were of course always standard gauge

A difficulty in his new job was that the only lodging he could find was at a farm located some four miles from the shed, but the farmer and his wife were friendly and Henry was able to help them out, with his invaluable experience from his own family farm. The farmer's wife knew very well what sustenance a labourer needed and Henry's lunch was the envy of most of his colleagues; and yet there was no danger of him putting on weight. Cleaning work did not encourage corpulence on the Great Western, nor any other, railway. The eight miles a day he had to walk took some getting used to, but only in the winter snow and ice did he find this a real trial.

Henry found his new duties stimulating. Oxford was short of firemen and, although he was technically a cleaner, much of his work was firing to Driver Jem Fordyce: an elderly driver in his mid-sixties, who had been driving the big engines for over twenty-five years. Driver Fordyce was no longer in the best of health but, being so experienced and knowledgeable, he had been kept on by the company and relieved from arduous duties on the main line. His reduced duties kept him – and consequently Henry – mostly on the local branch lines to Fairford, Blenheim and Woodstock, and Abingdon. This suited Henry very well as he felt very much at home among these small farming communities.

Henry made a further discovery: the broad gauge enginemen, virtually without exception, had a low opinion of the 'narrow' gauge. For them, the seven-foot gauge was the only sensible option and they could not see why any reasonable person failed to appreciate this. For a driver and fireman used to the broad gauge, to be sent north to Birmingham or Wolverhampton on a standard gauge train was felt to be a reprimand for some misdemeanour. By this time, the route between Paddington and Wolverhampton was already mixed gauge and in fact broad gauge trains were now rare north of Oxford.

Henry was also curious as to why the original seven foot had been increased by a quarter of an inch. He was enlightened by a permanent-way ganger: apparently the extra quarter-inch allowed more sideways movement to the wheel treads, thus producing a smoother ride over the points. Now that he fired on both broad and 'narrow' (as he had learned to call it) gauge types of engines, Henry was quickly persuaded of the superiority of Brunel's track, although he well knew that this was also due to its expensive and fastidious maintenance. He was now a confirmed broad gauge man.

5 - Problems in Gloucester (February 1867)

On occasions in Oxford, Henry Denton noticed that there were sometimes difficulties at the station when passengers heading for Shrewsbury, Chester or Birkenhead changed off broad gauge trains from stations like Penzance and Exeter in the South West, or from Cardiff in South Wales. The nuisance of having to retrieve their luggage from the broad gauge train and pack it into a northern standard gauge train caused a great many grumbles. However, he did not give the matter much thought until the time he was directed south to Didcot, where he and Driver Abraham Laughton took on a South Wales train as far as Gloucester. Henry was now on firing duties regularly (although he still only received a cleaner's pay).

At Gloucester, Midland Railway trains from Birmingham to Bristol on the standard gauge made connections with broad gauge Great Western trains for South Wales. Henry had heard that confusion on the long, single platform was the norm and the passengers involved were highly indignant at the failure of both companies to better deal with the situation. (Indeed, an illustration of the chaos had appeared as early as 1848 in the *Illustrated London News*.) Although things were no longer as bad as they had been then, Henry understood how confusion could arise in the transfer from one company to another, compounded by the need to change gauge instead of simply handing the trains over to the rival company, as was normal practice elsewhere.

Passengers could change trains by walking, but freight was a very different matter. The transhipment of goods was far more complex, time-consuming, and consequently expensive. He began to realise why the Gauge Commissioners had decided twenty years earlier that all future railways were to be built to the standard gauge of four feet and eight-and-a-half inches, for the sake of unity and cost.

His appreciation of passenger dissatisfaction was strengthened one day when he viewed for himself the chaos that could arise. It had been a dreadful winter's day of rain and hail, not to mention the zero temperature, even at midday. Henry's stint on the footplate of the twenty-year-old engine – a 4-2-2 with eight-foot driving wheels named *Swallow* – as it slowly steamed, apparently reluctantly, into the station at Gloucester, had been a worrying trial, even to a lad brought up on a farm and out in all weathers. Their footplate had no protection from the rain and hail.

Once under the limited protection of the platform canopy, Abraham Laughton removed his woollen balaclava headgear and once more took up his driver's top hat, which he had stored carefully in a special leather bag. He felt that, as a senior driver, the hat endowed him with a certain dignity, but it was rather impractical, given the kind of weather they had experienced on the run from Oxford. Now they were at the platform among the travelling public, Driver Laughton felt that his dignity and status needed to be re-imposed.

Henry was wearing a heavy pea jacket, which had provided some warmth but had rather inhibited his ability to fire, although his driver blamed the condition of the engine rather than his firing. He had driven with Cleaner Denton often enough to know him for a reliable and competent worker. Henry had not, of course, reached the driver's hat status, and normally wore a simple cap.

A number of passengers left the standard gauge train to catch a connection on the broad gauge to South Wales and began to move along the platform and wait there. A station porter announced that the waiting train to Cardiff and Swansea would be leaving as soon as the Midland Railway connecting train from Birmingham had arrived. Several passengers pleaded with a GWR official to allow the Cardiff train to leave on time, as the temperature on the station platform was hardly above freezing point. However, the official was adamant that the regulations were to be strictly observed and the South Wales train would only depart once the Midland train had arrived.

It was another half-hour before the Birmingham train belatedly made its way in and, as it gradually slowed, its carriage doors began to open and passengers began to pour out with their bags, parcels and cases clutched tightly. The passengers waiting to board the train – also with their luggage items – began to struggle against the flow of those descending from the carriages. The conflicting efforts of both groups began to show the makings of a series of minor confrontations. Mothers with their children struggled to keep hold of their offspring and their chattels: large, elderly ladies determinedly protected their huge hat boxes and sought comfortable forward-facing seats in the train at the same time. Fathers tried to force a way for their families through the congestion, occasionally meeting other equally aggressive fathers moving in the opposite direction.

Henry watched all this with increasing concern, wondering why the officials of both railway companies did not intervene, to assist in sorting out the chaos. As he observed the crowd, he noticed one young lady struggling with a girl in tears. He immediately moved into the rabble – by this time no other word was a suitable description – to try and assist them.

"Can I be of assistance, madam?" he asked the young lady as he stood next to her, holding a large gentleman out of her way.

"Oh, thank you, sir!" she replied in a strong Welsh accent. "We're trying to reach the Cardiff train. Myfanwy's da will be waiting there to meet us and take us on up the Rhonda. But we cannot move in this dreadful crush!"

Henry picked up their two cases and called over his shoulder to the lady, "Follow me, then, and I'll lead you to the Cardiff train."

He pushed his way through the crowd, looking from time

to time behind to see that they were able to follow him, until they all arrived safely at the platform where the Cardiff train was waiting. He saw them into seats, handed their cases to them, lifted his cap, and departed, their thanks sounding in his ears.

On his return, he saw Abraham Laughton grinning at him from their cab. "I noticed that you picked an attractive young lady to give your help to," he smiled. "At your age I would have done the same."

"But the chaos here makes life so difficult for our passengers, Mr Laughton," Henry complained. "Why does the company not do something to make their change of trains easier?"

"The Great Western sees this part of the country as their own area and they don't want to see the Midland encroaching any further than Bristol," replied his driver, "so they refuse to make changing companies' trains more convenient. They hope that the passengers from the Midland will give up and take GWR trains from Birmingham."

Henry nodded. "Oh I see," he replied, thinking how disappointing it was that great railway companies should be so petty when it came to serving their passengers' convenience.

Once they had serviced and turned their engine, they ran back to the station for their return trip to Didcot, where they could hand over to a London crew. They had half an hour to wait for their train from Swansea and when it arrived it was full. Many passengers hurried out with their baggage, heading for their train. One stout, well-dressed gentleman was accompanied by a liveried servant carrying his luggage. Clearly a man of the quality, mused Henry.

A small boy was sitting on a suitcase and the stout gentleman flicked out his glove as he passed, hitting the boy in the face.

"Hoy!" came an angry shout from a man returning to the boy, a loaf of bread in his hand. "What did you do that for?"

"The rascal was in my way!" said the gentleman indignantly.

"Well," replied the man; presumably boy's father, "you're in my way, too!" And with those words, he pushed the gentleman aside.

The liveried servant hurried to his master and made for the boy's father, while the gentleman called out, "Police!"

Two policemen standing at the end of the platform rushed over to separate the two fighting men.

One of the policemen took the servant by the arm. "Leave this to us, if you please," he said, while the second, larger policeman seized the father, growling, "You're causing a breach of the peace, fellow. You'll come with us." The little boy started howling as he saw his dad being hauled away by the two policemen, and Henry saw how the stout gentleman slipped what looked very like a gold sovereign into the hand of one of the policemen, who thanked him profusely.

"Did you see that, Mr Laughton?" Henry spoke with deep anger in his voice.

"Yes, I did," replied his driver. "Unfortunately, there is nothing we can do about it. The gentleman has the peelers on his side. He is obviously an important person and his word means far more than ours in a court of law."

"But what about the child?" asked Henry. "Is there nothing we can do for that boy?"

Driver Laughton looked at Henry, "What would you suggest? We have a train to drive; hundreds of passengers are relying on us."

Just then, an elderly lady went over to the boy to comfort him. "There," said Driver Laughton, "the boy looks to be in good hands. Now, let's get this train on the move."

Henry was preoccupied on the run back, although not sufficiently to cause inattention to his firing. He was unusually quiet at the station stops and his driver decided not to interrupt his fireman's thoughts. The lad was a country boy at heart and unused to the crude and uncouth ways of city life. Abe Laughton felt sorry for him but knew that Henry had to get used to the way things worked in the cities. The police often sided with the quality and there was little the lower orders could do about it. You just had to accept it, get on with your life, and try and stay out of trouble.

Henry was unaware that the GWR management had already decided (with great reluctance) that the broad gauge had to go. The gauge difference was becoming increasingly inconvenient for the company and they had been forced to compromise by adding a third, standard gauge rail to many routes, including to Paddington itself, to allow 'narrow' gauge through trains into routes previously restricted to the broad gauge.

But progress on re-gauging the GWR network was very slow. The company was in dire financial straits and the appointment in 1865 of Daniel Gooch, their previous locomotive engineer, to chairmanship of the company was only now beginning to have positive results. Nevertheless, the continuous embarrassment at Gloucester in particular was seen as something to be urgently looked into, and the South Wales main line was the next major area to be considered for re-gauging.

"When do you think Oxford is likely to be converted to standard gauge, Mr Laughton?" Henry asked his driver. "I mean, when Oxford has no more broad gauge track – it's already got third standard gauge rails in place."

"You'd have to ask the clerks at Paddington, lad," Driver Laughton replied. "I have not heard, but it won't concern me much anyway. I'll be retiring from driving in a few years."

"But I much prefer the broad gauge," grumbled Henry.

"Well, I reckon you have a few more years yet, but let me give you a word of advice, young Denton. Try for a transfer to a station on the main line to the west. They won't be able to change that until the rest of the system has been converted."

Henry nodded, glad that at least he was still able to look forward to several years yet on the broad gauge. And applying for a transfer was a good thought.

6 - Life in a running shed
(July 1868)

Cleaner Denton was settling down in Oxford whilst keeping an eye on the progress of the third, additional rail to the original broad gauge track on the GWR system. He was thinking of applying for a transfer to somewhere that would give him a longer career on the broad gauge. Meanwhile, he was finding out about some of the unexpected details concerning life in the cab of a steam locomotive.

One horrific accident gave him a very sharp reminder of the dangers which enginemen were exposed to in pursuit of their duty. It was occasionally necessary for enginemen to move around the footplate while the train was in motion, in order to pick up any problems so that smooth running could be maintained without having to stop, and thus lose time: this was especially important on a passenger train. Passengers tended to become irate if their train was not on time and this often brought complaints to management, invariably followed by demands on the engine crew for an explanation. If management was not satisfied, pay could be docked and the details recorded for future consideration when promotion was in the offing.

Most Oxford men were disappointed if they were rostered on a northbound train as such duties were normally on the standard gauge, which Parliament had decreed for all future railway building. But the standard gauge trackwork did not yet match the quality of the broad, although its permanent-way engineers were making marked improvements to it.

Driver Joseph Barnes was a very promising young driver, with an air of complete confidence in his skill on the footplate. Most of the time, his belief in his ability was justified, yet on one occasion this belief was coloured by overconfidence. On the day in question, they were running a short, four-coach express to Wolverhampton and the engine – a usually reliable 0-4-2 – was giving off the dreaded burning smell and the emission of blue smoke from lack of lubrication from the running gear.

"Dan," Driver Barnes said to his fireman, "keep her running while I check the motion, it needs a drop more oil."

The two men had a good working partnership and Dan Hartley often took over the driving for a short stint. He did so now with an affirmative nod. The fire was burning nicely, allowing Dan to concentrate on his driving.

Joe took the oilcan and proceeded to work his way along the front of the footplate, where he could check the motion. Leaning forward, he tipped the spout of the oil can onto the bearing of the big end under the boiler and applied a small amount of oil. He moved further forwards, to drop a little more oil on the internal crosshead bearing and then the cylinder lubricator oil cups in front of the smokebox. Nodding to himself in satisfaction, he straightened up to return to his place at the rear. But he had forgotten the vital principle that it was essential to keep hold of the handrail when moving about the footplate of a running engine.

The engine lurched over a poorly aligned rail joint and Joe lost his balance, falling off the front of the engine onto the track, and was instantly killed as the train ran over his body. A shocked Dan Hartley eased the train to a halt, applied the engine brake, and ran to the back of the train, where he saw Joe's decapitated body. He hurried to inform Guard Sanders, who looked out and saw the fireman.

"Why have we stopped, Dan?"

"Driver Barnes has been run over! He was oiling the motion and fell off the front of the engine!"

"Good god!"

They both quickly examined the remains of the driver's body. The track looked like the shambles in the back of a butcher's shop; several body parts were scattered over the three rails.

"Has someone been injured?" came a voice from the rear carriage. "I am a medical man. Perhaps I can be of assistance?"

A well-dressed man of mature years clambered down onto the track, approached the two men, and noticed the state of affairs.

"Ah, I see." He carefully examined the situation. "No, gentlemen. I'm afraid that any help I can give would only be of a formal nature, confirming death. Hmm... I never saw anything quite like that even in '54 in the Crimea. However," he added, "you might best be advised to get the train back in motion before you have half your passengers out and gazing in horrified fascination at this scene. It would be much better all round if they were not to witness this. I will remain here, on watch as it were, until you can order officials from the nearest station."

"Can you drive us on, Dan?" asked Guard Sanders, assuming his responsibility as custodian of the train

"Yes, I can do that," replied the shaken fireman.

The guard turned to the medical man. "Your name, sir?"

"Dr Smethers, of St Mary's Hospital."

"The Great Western Railway is deeply obliged to you, sir," said the guard, writing down the details.

There was deep sadness at Oxford Shed; everyone had liked Joe Barnes, but they all knew that he had taken one risk too many. Any engineman on the running plate of a moving engine was well aware of the dangers of not holding on securely if they had to leave the cab.

Henry discovered another unexpected facet of life in a running shed, concerning an increase, albeit unofficial, of one's pay. The coal usage of all drivers was carefully recorded and those who were able to manage with less than was allowed for a journey were rewarded with a pay bonus. Conversely, those who used more had to pay for the extra.

Ambrose Bolton was a coal office clerk with a penchant for putting some of his meagre pay on dubious horses from time to time, and frequently complained of how the nags seemed to deprive him of his anticipated earnings. Yet in spite of this he appeared to manage his pay very well. Henry was puzzled: if the man lost his bets so consistently, why did he always seem to have enough to continue his failures?

It was many months before he found the answer. Ambrose, it seemed, was popular with a few of the senior drivers in the shed – those who were given the plum jobs with the best locomotives and top passenger expresses because of their experience and driving skill. This, thought Henry, was curious, as the senior drivers generally kept themselves aloof from those they regarded as the lower orders, in the social organisation of a running shed. Stores clerks were indisputably of that ilk.

One morning during his lunch break, Henry overheard a short conversation between Ambrose and a very senior driver; this took place behind an engine left on the scrap siding.

"Can't help yer with more'n a hundredweight over yer limit this time, Mr Beckinsale," said Ambrose quietly. "The stores foreman is gettin' suspicious an' checkin' me books careful, like."

"That's fine, Ambrose; but I'll be wanting a bit more next time, when your foreman settles down again." Glancing through a gap between the wheels and the bottom of the boiler of the old locomotive, Henry thought he saw the glint of a half-sovereign changing hands. Half an hour later, he noticed another senior driver having a quiet word with Ambrose. He was surprised and disappointed; he had assumed the senior drivers were above such offences.

Walking on, he was further disillusioned, when he passed a closed van in which he heard muttering. Glancing inside through a gap in the planking, Henry was shocked to see shaking white buttocks beneath a hitched-up dress: it was Ambrose's daughter earning her sixpences. He had heard she was offering minor services to enginemen but had supposed it was to do with laundry help; clearly it was of a more physical nature. He shook his head in disappointment; he had always assumed the senior men, regarded as pillars of society, were above reproach. Now he knew that, in the right circumstances, they could be just as venal as anybody else.

Driver Seth Burton was a senior driver with a difference. He was a man with whom Henry Denton got on very well.

Seth was friendly, good-natured, and willing to give his younger charges whatever assistance he felt they required. Yet how he managed to remain a senior driver was a matter that caused Henry a great deal of head-scratching. Seth seemed to have an unceasing range of minor errors to commit in his driving. Every mistake cost him a fine and this occurred at least once a month. On the occasions when Henry found himself firing to Driver Burton, he worried that he would also be included in that incident and have the misdemeanour recorded in his own file.

The first time he was rostered to fire to Driver Burton, they were appointed to shunting duties in Oxford Yard, which was of mixed gauge. Here, both drivers and shunters had to be careful about which tracks they were working on. Most trackwork was dual gauge but even here there were a few sets of points which were single gauge only – they switched only one of the two gauges. The men were to marshal a rake of empty wagons ready for another crew to take to North Wales collieries, to be filled with coal and returned to locomotive sheds between Birmingham and Oxford on the standard gauge.

They gathered the wagons and set them up on a long siding, ready for the train engine to collect for the run to the north. Driver Burton called to a shunter to set the point for them to run back to the station for their next duty.

"The long siding's broad gauge only, sir," came the shouted reply. Although Oxford Yard had mixed gauge track, the long siding they had moved onto was only standard gauge for ten yards, enough for an engine to reverse into.

But Driver Burton was explaining the move to Henry and waved to the shunter to set the points, ignoring the warning.

Shunter Sefton therefore assumed that Driver Burton was only going as far as the very short standard gauge section of the long siding, which allowed standard gauge engines to reverse into a loop leading to the shed.

The driver heard the clunk of the point lever going over and the click of the point blades, and surged ahead, assuming they would proceed along the loop line.

Henry was listening earnestly to his driver and did not notice where they were heading until the engine suddenly lurched to one side and came to an abrupt stop with a hiss of escaping steam.

"We're off the road!" muttered Seth Burton in despair. "Why didn't that addle-pated shunter warn me?"

"Umm – he did shout something, Mr Burton, when you were telling me about today's duty, though I didn't catch what he said," murmured Henry apologetically.

Driver Burton sighed, "That will cost me a pretty penny!" he said. "The shed foreman will reduce my pay again! But don't worry, young Denton, this is my responsibility alone. There will not be any record against your name. It was entirely my fault."

Re-railing an engine that had come off the road was common in the yards and around most sheds. The trackwork here did not carry the most important traffic – passengers – and movements were normally slow: light engines moved to and fro, and shunting was carried on at a fairly slow speed. Consequently, the railway companies were reluctant to spend money on high quality maintenance of this type or track; they assumed that their employees would take care to keep their charges on the rails.

The shed fitters soon had the matter well in hand but the shedmaster was not amused. "Last month, Driver Burton, you were fined for snatching at a freight and breaking a coupling. That cost you a shilling's loss of pay; now you have derailed an engine, which will cost you another two shillings! I'm thinking that what I'll have to do is to pay you nothing except for a daily rate of thruppence for every day you don't do anything silly." He shook his head. "For Pete's sake, Seth, try and go a month without a fine. That would make a nice change. And," he added as an afterthought, "perhaps I will pair you regularly with young Cleaner Denton. He seems to have his head screwed on."

7 - Under London on the broad gauge (September 1868)

"I'm almost a fireman now, Mother!" Henry's proud boast made his mother smile. The boy had blossomed since leaving farm work and joining the railway service. Mr and Mrs Denton had long got over their disappointment at not having their son take over the farm. On this score, they had been lucky in that Elijah Wingate, the man who had taken Henry's place as farm worker six years previously, was a hard worker. Elijah had, right from the start, shown immediate enthusiasm for the work, was highly competent, and fully able to look after the farm whenever the Dentons left to visit relatives, or to shop for a few days in Chester, the county capital. Mr Denton had even hinted to Elijah that, when the time came, he and his wife would be prepared to listen with a sympathetic ear to Elijah buying the farm, should he ever be in a position to raise the necessary capital.

But the Dentons' pleasure was undiluted as their son had travelled north to see them; even though this was accompanied by the sad news that he had moved further away from them, to Oxford. They had not seen their lad for three years, although he had regularly kept in touch by letter. Mrs Denton had lovingly retained his letters with their envelopes (it was only thirty years later that this habit of hers produced a surprising dividend: Henry had kept all her letters and a friend pointed out that the Penny Black stamps on the envelopes were now of some considerable value.)

"I am very pleased for you, dear," said Mrs Denton, eyeing the boy's muscled arms. "The work seems to be building you up. Are you eating enough?"

"Indeed I am, Mother! Now, though, I had to find some new digs in Oxford. I've been lucky so far with landladies and hope to continue my good fortune."

"What new turns of duty do you have to do, son?" asked his father.

"I'm a cleaner, Father, but they let me fire quite a lot, mostly up to Reading and Didcot and back, but sometimes as far as London," replied Henry with pride. "Paddington Station has been rebuilt and is much bigger than it was; I've been there a couple of times already. It's an exciting place to be and sometimes I expect to have two or three hours to look around there, and can even get to the shops on Oxford Street. I've heard that they have wonderful things in them, but of course everything is far too expensive for me. In any case," he added, "they won't really have anything I need."

"Paddington, eh?" asked his father. "Then might you have time to look at the history of the city?"

"That depends on the return trip, Father. Sometimes we only have an hour to service the engine and return. Why, what had you in mind?"

"I've only been to London once. When I was a child, my parents took me there and they showed me the Tower of London. It was grand! You should visit it."

"I will if I get the opportunity."

Some months later, this opportunity arose. Henry and Driver Seth Burton were put on a Paddington and return roster with a two-hour turn-around at the terminus. It was raining heavily in London when they arrived mid-morning and as Seth slowly backed their Waverley 4-4-0 engine *Lalla Rookh* into the shed for servicing, he stumbled and fell towards the backhead. As he raised his head, he knocked the regulator, moving it upwards. Instead of slowing, the engine lurched and hit the buffers smartly, doing minor damage to its own buffers.

A fitter was called in to assess the damage but said that he could have it fixed overnight, once the paperwork was cleared by the shed foreman. The two Oxford enginemen had to find their own night's accommodation, paid for by Seth, who accepted the blame with a shrug. It was a situation he was used to.

While Henry was disappointed at the setback, he realised that he now had time to explore some of what the city had to offer, recalling his father's recommendation to visit the Tower. He arranged to meet his driver again that evening at the accommodation, giving him the rest of the day to explore the city. One of the porters informed him that from Paddington he could catch another train across the city, terminating not too far from his destination. Henry nodded in thanks and was intrigued to discover that it was not only underground but also broad gauge.

But as the east-bound train to the city pulled in at the platform at Paddington, Henry noticed that the passenger train was a Great Northern Railway standard gauge train.

"Must be pleasant to be driving under cover with the rain outside drenching everyone else!" he called to the driver. "I'm an Oxford fireman and we usually get soaked in weather like this."

"Wrong, young fella," replied the driver, grinning. "You say 'pleasant'? Wait till yer get ter the City an' then see wot yer fink."

Puzzled at this remark, Henry climbed into one of the carriages and sat down to enjoy this unusual ride. The carriage was full of passengers and by the time the train had travelled no more than about fifteen minutes, Henry had begun to think that the driver had a point. The air, already rather stuffy when he got in, had now become foul. The windows were very small and up near the roof. Several passengers were smoking and the steam and smoke from the locomotive was entering the carriage, adding to the problem. It became impossible to see clearly; yet none of the other passengers seemed to be unduly concerned.

"Is the air in this train always like this, sir?" Henry asked the old gentleman sitting next to him.

"Not at all," replied the gentleman. "Today we are fortunate; some days it is quite difficult to breathe."

"Do you use this train often, then?"

"Why yes, every day, young man. I work in a bank in the City."

"And you have to breathe in this atmosphere every day?"

"Certainly; my alternative is to travel by omnibus, which requires an hour and a half; I would need to sit for three hours each day in cramped and smelly conditions. The train takes a mere forty minutes."

Henry began to wonder whether a visit to the Tower was really worth the next half-hour of choking. Being once a farm lad, he decided that he would walk back to Paddington, no matter how long it took. There was a slight easing of the fug as the train passed from the tunnel into an open-air section towards the end of the line. He got out gratefully at Farringdon Street and paused at the engine to speak to the driver once more. The fireman had climbed down to uncouple the carriages as the driver watched the departing passengers. His clothing now was soaked from the rain.

"I understand what you mean now, sir," said Henry to the driver.

"Yerse, I'd rather get pissed on by the rain than smoked aht in these tunnels!" cackled the driver, "but this 'ere's me duty fer the nex' two monfs."

Henry nodded and when he reached the open air and heavy rain outside the station and, breathing in gratefully, turned his steps towards the Tower.

In spite of the weather, Henry was deeply impressed by the Tower and its history; he admired the suits of armour and paused at the spot where the scaffold had been, musing at the executions which had been carried out there. He had never understood how Christians could accept both the Fifth Commandment and the execution of criminals in a country which ostensibly claimed to follow Christian values. A few months earlier, he had been invited to join colleagues to watch the public execution at Newgate prison. "Last chance, Henry, to watch the Tyburn jig," he had been told. He had refused. He had never been convinced of the value of such killing and in any case the reported behaviour of the mobs ("My, my, he's going to die!" was the mocking chant) at these events had always disgusted him.

He had been longer at the Tower than anticipated and realised that he had to get back to Paddington quickly, in order to rejoin Driver Burton at the arranged time. He no longer had sufficient time to walk the whole distance and reluctantly boarded another underground train back to Paddington. It was again full and just as stuffy as on his first run. Henry decided that a normal footplate in the open weather was far preferable to choking in the foul atmosphere of an underground train.

Seth Burton greeted him when they met at their overnight accommodation. "How was the Tower then, lad?"

"I found the Tower quite admirable," replied Henry, "but the underground train journey was most uncomfortable."

"Yes, I have done it myself once: I'll not be doing it again," agreed his driver, pulling a newspaper from his pocket and pointing to a column in it. "There'll be no more public executions at Tyburn," he said.

"Really?" asked Henry in surprise.

"No, the writer of this article states that the government is considering conducting them only in prisons to which the public will not be invited to observe."

"But why is that? They are very popular."

"Yes, but they cause too much public disorder."

"Well, that's certainly true."

Promptly at seven the next morning, the two men were at Paddington Shed, looking over their locomotive, which had been repaired overnight as promised. Next to it was an old 4-2-2 named *Sultan* on a local passenger; one of these locomotives had represented the broad gauge case in 1848, when the Gauge Commissioners were debating the merits of the different gauges. It had run at over sixty miles per hour, reinforcing the claim of the high speeds attainable with the wider gauge.

On this occasion, their run was uneventful as far as Slough, and Henry was secretly disappointed that there was no reason to see whether 60mph was warranted. They were informed there that there had been an accident near

Maidenhead; a coal train had lost some of its load, which was scattered across the down line ahead of them. They would need to proceed very slowly and carefully past the men shovelling coal back into the wagons. This held them up and Henry smiled to himself as they eased their way past the scene of the accident. Driver Burton would need to put some speed on if they were to arrive at Oxford on time. Perhaps he would see if the engine would manage 60 mph again.

"We're going to have to put a spurt on, Henry, if we want to be punctual. You'll have to put your back into the firing." Seth Burton, like all drivers, disliked being late, as it could affect his pay packet. Henry nodded. He had expected a fast run and was now looking forward to it.

"Fine by me, Mr Burton," he called, as he bent to scoop up more coal. Seth Burton opened the throttle and as they hurried into Reading Henry soon found their speed exhilarating. A stop here held them only briefly but they were still well behind time. Turning north towards Didcot, they accelerated quickly and Henry had to hold on to the handrail tightly when he was not firing.

Seth Burton looked at him with a grin; "The old kettle can still do it," he shouted, thus distracting his fireman and at the same time failing to see the stop signal and the frantic waving flag of the bobby. The busily shovelling Henry did not see it, either.

Hurtling round a curve, the horrified driver saw the rear of slow-moving goods train in front of them. They hit the brake van and wagons of the freight, derailing both their own engine and the last half-dozen wagons. Driver Burton was thrown off the footplate into the field and hit his head on a stone. Henry was able to cling on to the rail and, although not seriously injured, was badly shaken. The guard in the brake van was also hurt. The driver's inattention at a critical moment had not only injured several people, damaging rolling stock, but had left him concussed.

Driver Burton, it seemed, had made his last careless error.

8 - Pride comes before a fall (April 1869)

Henry Denton had been disappointed yet relieved at losing his driver; he had liked Driver Burton but conceded that the man had been a liability to the railway company. This could not be said of his new driver, Lawrence Parkinson, however. Driver Parkinson was an easy-going man who gave his firemen every encouragement; something that Henry relished. After about three weeks, the driver began to see that Henry knew his stuff and could be relied upon to do what was required of a fireman. He therefore began to give Henry increasing responsibilities, showing him how to handle the regulator with appropriate care and how to anticipate how fast to drive, depending on the state of the engine and the track. Wet track required extra care in using the brakes and the driver had to rely on his accumulated experience.

When shunting in Oxford Yard, Driver Parkinson sometimes told Henry to take over the regulator for short transfer runs in the locality while he himself took over the firing duties, carefully keeping an eye on Henry's driving at the same time. Gradually, Henry developed a feel for what the locomotive could do, and what was unwise to expect of it. He also grew in self-confidence when handling the regulator and the brake, which required careful anticipation on the short runs, while not forgetting that he was not yet a fireman. Nevertheless, his familiarity with life on the footplate increased, with work on both broad and 'narrow gauge' engines. He was often on runs to Didcot and Banbury and once even fired with Driver Parkinson to Reading and return. On slow goods trains, on the longer stretches between stations, Lawrence would take over the shovel and step aside on the footplate to allow Henry to handle the regulator for a few miles, switching back wherever a signal bobby might see them.

The bobbies were still to be seen on the trackside locations where the new semaphore signals had not yet replaced the old disc and crossbar signals. The bobby would show a white flag to indicate that the way ahead was clear. A red flag indicated danger; the driver would wave in passing, to acknowledge that he had understood. But by now the new-fangled signal boxes were beginning to appear, to the relief of the bobbies, who could spend their time in comfort inside with a stove heater, which also served to brew their tea upon. Some enginemen were very envious until they learned how much effort was needed to move the heavy lever every time a point had to be changed. Signals were easier to change because they were counterbalanced.

Five months after Henry had been partnered with Lawrence Parkinson, he felt that he was really making progress with his driving skills. Driver Parkinson was giving him more turns on the regulator and 'learning the road' as it was called; even praising him to the shedmaster, informing the latter that in his opinion Henry would one day make a very competent driver.

"'E's still only a younker, sir, but I reckon 'e 'as the attitude the Great Western needs fer its drivers. 'E's allus on time fer 'is work an' 'e's powerful smart."

"Yes, I agree with your remarks, Driver Parkinson. I've noticed that Denton is keen and intelligent, and seems to be what we're looking for. Keep a close eye on him and we'll see what he can do in the months ahead."

Thus, things appeared to be going well for Henry; his only disappointment was to hear that the broad gauge line under London was being dismantled and the broad gauge in South Wales was also planned for conversion to standard gauge. He determined to stay as long as possible on broad gauge tracks. In the meantime, he would increase his experience on the footplate on either broad or standard gauge engines as much as he could, by learning from other drivers as well as Driver Parkinson.

One foggy morning, Henry found himself firing on an older engine shunting in Oxford Yard when Driver Parkinson decided that it was time Henry had another stint on the regulator. This older engine had what was called an 'iron coffin'; a narrow, upright metal hut at the back of the tender, designed for a porter to keep an eye on the train during journeys, to check that it had not parted and was still intact. Porter Samuel Fletcher, however, was out of sight, waiting by the coaches down a long siding, ready to be collected for the Reading local once it was marshalled.

While Driver Parkinson was busy checking the water level, Henry on the regulator – assuming that the porter was watching from the 'iron coffin' – backed the engine towards a siding holding these coaches some way down it. The siding, however, was not yet set correctly and Henry backed the engine into a rake of wagons stabled in the adjacent siding, derailing three of them.

"God's teeth, 'Enry, what've yer done?" Lawrence Parkinson looked up furiously from the water gauges and stared at the derailed wagons. "Didn't yer check that the points was set correctly?"

"I thought that Porter Fletcher was checking them from the tender, Mr Parkinson!" Henry was shocked and horrified at what had happened. He realised too late that the fault was his: he should have made certain that the points had been set to the siding with the carriages. He had been too cocky at his own ability and the confidence his superiors had shown in him. He should not have just assumed that Porter Fletcher (who was now hurrying towards them) had been on the tender; he should have checked.

Henry had made two major errors and nobody else could possibly be held responsible for them. He shook his head in despair.

There followed a painful interview in the shedmaster's office. Henry was fined one shilling: a sizeable sum on a cleaner's pay. He was also informed that he would be banned from practice driving any engine for the next six months.

"I believe, Cleaner Denton, that you will make a very competent engineman one day with the GWR, but your two errors today tell me that you have not yet absorbed the regulations pertaining to the need for care and attention to your important responsibilities. Work on the railway can easily kill people. You will no doubt recall what happened to Driver Joe Barnes; he was a good driver who made a simple mistake that cost him his life. A railwayman's life is always a dangerous one; more so than most passengers realise, and a simple error can also put many other lives at risk."

"Yes, sir." Henry's crestfallen face as he left the office showed that the shedmaster's words had struck home.

Driver Parkinson was called in next.

"We know who is really at fault here, Larry, don't we?"

"Yes, sir, I were too quick to give 'im the regulator without checkin' the points, which was me job."

"No, it wasn't. It's rather more important than that: you did not emphasize to him that the driver is always responsible for everything on the engine. You were still officially the driver, so you must take the blame. You are fined two shillings for allowing an untrained man to do something he was not ready for."

"Yes, sir."

"I agree with you that one day he'll make a fine engineman but he has to learn to take responsibility. Don't let him drive until next October. Have you got that?"

"I 'ave, sir."

It was a chastened Driver Parkinson who greeted his fireman the next morning. "I'm right mortal sorry, lad, but I've bin told yer not ter touch me regulator for six months, nor anyone else's, neither."

"I'm also very sorry that I got you into trouble with the shedmaster, Mr Parkinson. I don't know why I didn't remember to check the point blades before I moved the engine."

"Well, at least yer've seen fer yersel' 'ow things c'n go wrong when yer in charge of a great engine! Now 'ere's a question for ye: Oo's the best driver in our shed?"

Henry paused and thought for a minute or two. "I would say that would be Driver Green, Driver Thwaites, or perhaps Driver Hopkins?"

"Aye, I reckon it would be one of 'em. Well, if you was

to catch a look in their pers'nal records, would you see anythin' like what you did yestern?"

"Good heavens, no!" Henry was startled at this thought. "They're very good and careful drivers and they have years of experience."

"Right agen, lad. But let me tell ye that Jeb Green once took a local train right through Didcot platform before he realized 'e should've stopped there. 'E was goin' too fast ter stop. 'E 'ad ter back 'is train up agen. 'E were lucky; they on'y fined 'im one shillin' an' sixpence.

"Driver Green did that?"

"Aye, an' 'Arry Thwaites fell asleep on 'is engine - 'e were on a long shift, mind ye - when 'e were still a fireman and let 'is fire out. 'E were lucky 'e could rekindle the embers agen before the foreman saw it."

"Yes, but—"

"An' Sam 'Opkins - yer gotta laugh - seven year back it were now, fell off 'is engine in a tunnel when 'e fell over 'is fireman's shovel. They was only goin' slow at the time. That cost 'im two shillin'."

"Driver Parkinson, are you pulling my leg?"

"No younker, I'm tellin' yer the truth. But don't you breathe a word of what I've tol' yer. Specially about Jeb Green. 'E's a big fella, an' if'n 'e finds out what I tell'd yer, I'll be wantin' a bed in a 'orspital."

Henry could hardly believe what his driver was telling him; these were important mistakes or errors of judgement which could have had serious consequences. And they had been made by the best drivers in the shed!

"An' I'll tell yer summat else, too," continued Driver Parkinson. "There 'aint no engineman in the shed what 'asn't 'ad somethin' similar on 'is sheet."

"Then how can I make sure I don't make such an error again, Mr Parkinson?"

"Ye can't. Nobody's perfect, lad. Ye'll just 'ave ter learn the rules and keep 'em. If'n yer keep doin' that, they'll finally stay in yer 'ead an' ye'll make a good driver. Even the shedmaster ses that; 'e tole me so 'isself."

For the next six months, Henry took this advice to heart and, although he was disappointed not to be able to take a brief turn on the regulator, he persevered with his firing and his attitude. He worked on both broad and standard gauge engines and on goods and local passenger trains around the Oxford area. He learned the road from Banbury in the north and as far as Reading in the south. He fired older 2-2-2 engines of the Star class, with no weather protection whatsoever, at the same time admiring their huge, polished brass steam domes. One morning, he was delighted to learn that he was to fire an 0-6-0 engine with small five-foot driving wheels. The engine was called *Chester*, after his boyhood home town. GWR broad gauge engines did not have numbers, only names.

He did not appreciate the 4-4-0ST saddle tank engines, with their huge water tanks laid over the boiler; they looked to him to be disproportioned somehow, and it could be difficult to see ahead over the tanks.

He fired occasionally northwards on the standard gauge, with one thrilling evening in November on a Paddington to Birkenhead express. He had been waiting at Reading for a return to Oxford when the fireman of the express was caught sipping from a bottle of beer and was instantly dismissed. Henry knew the road to Wolverhampton so was able to take over the Sir Daniel class 2-2-2 express engine that had brought the train from Paddington. He still preferred the broad gauge but had to admit that firing a standard gauge express locomotive could also be a thrilling experience.

On his return to Oxford, he was called into the shedmaster's office, where he was informed that a glowing report on his duty had been sent in. As a consequence, it was felt that he could be permitted to resume practice driving under the watchful eye of his driver once more.

He had, it seemed, atoned for his error.

9 - A Cornish complication
(November 1871)

The following few months at Oxford were for Henry both stimulating and challenging. He was more careful in his duties and, as before, earned the approbation of all those he worked with. He also found himself entrusted with an increasing level of shunting and main line work. Both duties included sessions of driving under the ever watchful eye of Driver Parkinson, who knew that his own supervision was in turn observed by the shedmaster. Nevertheless, Henry was gradually expanding his experience of railway work, which once more included limited driving.

One day in late October, Henry received a disturbing letter from his parents. His father's sister Annie, who had married a Cornishman and moved to Truro many years earlier, had become seriously ill. His father wondered whether Henry could travel to Cornwall and find out more.
  Henry approached the shedmaster with the request for a week's leave so that he could visit his aunt; he had not had any leave for many months and could perhaps expect a sympathetic response.
  "How curious that you should wish to visit Truro," the shedmaster remarked. "I think we can do better than a week's leave, however. The West Cornwall Railway is having problems finding footplatemen and the Great Western is in a position to assist. I could send you there on duty for a month."
"That would be excellent, sir," said Henry. "I could see my aunt and report her condition to my parents."

One week later, Henry had seen his aunt, discovering she was not as ill as his parents had been led to believe, and uncle, and his hitherto unknown cousins, and was ensconced in their house in Truro.

He had also reported to the West Cornwall Railway Officer in Truro, who was pleased to see him. Henry was surprised to discover that the railway had been standard gauge but had added a third, broad gauge rail to the line and that passengers from London were now able to travel from Paddington to Penzance without having to change trains at Truro.

He was expecting to have a little difficulty with understanding some of his colleagues because many spoke with such a strong West Country accent, but he was startled to discover an additional problem in his work on the footplate. In Oxford he was used to working on both broad and narrow gauge trains but on the West Cornwall he had certainly not anticipated firing on a goods train which had both broad and standard gauge vehicles in it.

"What?" he exclaimed. "Broad and narrow gauge vehicles in the same train?"

"Ar well, 'Enry," said Driver Lowan Trelawney on his first run to Penzance with such a train. "We wuz allus a Stephenson's gauge railway, but now yer Associated Companies is 'elpin' uz, we 'az ter put a broad rail in so's yer big trains can run through ter Penzance."

"But why have standard gauge wagons at all?" queried Henry.

"That's so the shipyards at 'Ayle an' Truro can still send their wagons around the system; they was built ter the Stephenson's gauge ter begin with an' some of the tracks was never changed."

Henry learned that when a mixed gauge train was assembled there had to be converter wagons between the vehicles of different gauges, to allow for the varying spacings between the buffers. There were broad gauge wagons with extra-long wooden buffers mounted, to permit the buffing of vehicles of both gauges. This meant that the staff had to check that the trains so assembled were directed only onto mixed gauge track.

Initially, Henry thought that this sounded easy, as mixed gauge track shared points onto sidings, but he soon realized that the points leading to a mixed gauge siding were sometimes quite separate. This meant that a train containing vehicles of both gauges could not use it without much shunting and reforming. Marshalling such trains generally gave rise to considerable frustration (and inventive vocabulary) from those involved. The buffers of the older vehicles were merely wooden blocks, although metal sprung buffers were beginning to become the norm, to reduce damage done in the course of shunting.

One morning in Truro Yard, Henry was assisting a shunter who was marshalling a train for Penzance, and quietly swearing to himself; the shunting horse was skittish and sometimes tried to pull its wagons before the ropes were firmly fastened. He also found himself more than once stepping into the horse droppings.

Driver Trelawney smiled to himself when Henry finally climbed onto the footplate; the lad was going to have an interesting morning, he thought. "Well now, 'Enry me lad, yer in fer a treat."

"How's that then, Mr Trelawney?"

"This 'ere goods 'az ter be sorted. Some standard ve'cles 'az ter come from Portreath an' 'az ter go ter Penzance and some broads iz from Bristol fer Penzance; 'an ye'll need ter use yer nous a bit."

"Sounds fairly straightforward."

"Ye don't know the 'alf of it! Some sidin's 'ave mixed gauge access points an' some don't."

Henry thought about that for a moment then remarked, "Oh, I see what you mean. The marshalling is going to need much more care than usual." He had occasionally noticed that a broad gauge locomotive could, with caution, couple to a standard gauge wagon to move it. One had to position a long plank over the engine's buffers, to allow for the difference in buffer spacing.

"Now then young 'Enry, we'm goin' ter marshal the wagons for their destinations."

"Fine, Mr Trelawney." Henry watched as Lowan Trelawney drove the engine carefully, checking that his access to the waiting standard gauge wagons from

Newnham Yard was mixed gauge, and drove gently up to the wagons. Then he brought the engine to a stop clear of the train.

"Er – how do we get vehicles of different gauges into the same train?" asked Henry

"We 'ave to use one o' they converter wagons."

"Converter wagons?"

"Think about it; 'ow do yer couple wagons with different gauges?"

"I don't know. How?"

"Yer gets a converter wagon. It's got special coupling arrangements. It's broad gauge but it'll couple to a narrer gauge wagon."

"But the buffers are at different distances apart!"

"Ar, that's right, they are. But them converter wagons 'az very wide wooden buffers so they still buff up together."

"Sounds like a tricky business altogether."

"Yer learnin' fast, youngster."

The marshalling took far longer than normal because, apart from any other problems, some of the mixed gauge sidings had separate gauge access points, meaning that much shunting was needed to get the wagons sorted. They had to stop to pick up and drop off vehicles at both Camborne and at the junction for Hayle, and the run took far longer than Henry would have thought from the distance involved.

"Oi bain't fond o' mixed gauge trains," said Lowan, "Yer've gotta be on yer toes the 'ole way an' it's tirin'. An'," he added, "yer've got ter watch when the narrer gauge track changes from left to right within the broad gauge, as it sometimes does. I've got ter slow the train right down then ter give the narrer vehicles a chance to slide across."

Having once already spent a busy morning in Oxford dealing with standard gauge train on mixed gauge track, Henry could easily visualise the difficulties from the added complication of checking that their train had on mixed gauge tracks every inch of the way.

The run was indeed very tiring. Whenever they went through a small station, the standard gauge track switched across so that the passengers on standard gauge trains could alight at the platforms. There was at least one fright when the train was signalled into the yard and the driver almost derailed his train before Henry noticed that the access points were not mixed gauge and yelled a warning.

Luckily, Driver Trelawney had noticed it as well and braked in time to prevent an accident. They had to stop and break their train into its broad and standard gauge sections before they could enter. Driver Trelawney was extremely irate and demanded to know why the signal had been incorrectly set. He was only partly mollified to hear that there had been a failure to communicate between the signalling and the permanent way departments when the access points had been altered from broad to mixed gauge.

On a return run from Penzance to Truro to end their shift, they were held up by a signal check at Marazion.

Henry noticed Lowan Trelawney pulled a strange pastry out of his pocket. "What's that Mr Trelawaney?"

The driver held it up with a grin. "Oi 'az these fer me lunch sometimes," he said. "It's a pasty. It's remains of yestern's dinner wrapped up in pastry; very 'andy ter shove in yer pocket. There's spuds, carrots, turnips, peas or whatever yer missus 'az cooked, all mixed up and wrapped in a parcel. They's used in tin mines and the pastry's 'ard so's if'n yer drop em down the mineshaft, they doan break!"

Henry was unsure, looking at his driver's face whether to believe this latter statement or not. Nevertheless, it sounded like a good use of 'yestern's dinner', he thought, and decided to see if his landlady in Oxford could do something similar once he got back.

Henry's month in Truro soon passed and he was sorry to lose the company of this new branch of his family. He was less sorry to abandon the tricky work on the occasional mixed gauge trains, which even in West Cornwall were thankfully rare. He was further disappointed in Oxford on hearing from his friend Driver Lawrence Parkinson.

"If yer still like the broad gauge, 'Enry, yer might 'ave to ask fer a transfer. Oxford will be losin' the broad soon, I 'ear. They say that only the main line to the West will be left. An'," he added quietly, "I've 'eard that'll go an' all, as soon as Sir Daniel goes to 'is grave."

Henry read all he could find about the plans the GWR had for its future; he also decided to look further south for any reports of cleaners required on the main line to the west. He mentioned his interest to the Oxford shedmaster, who promised to keep an ear open for anything suitable. It was, however, several months before he called Henry into his office with some news.

"Cleaner Denton, I know you wish to stay on the broad gauge as long as possible, although I have to add that I regard you as a valuable company servant who could perhaps make a fine engineman, and I would be sad to see you go. There are two vacancies I have heard about. A fireman is needed in Westbury and a cleaner vacancy exists in Chippenham. My recommendation would be for you to apply to Chippenham. At Westbury, you would need to qualify as a fireman, but that route is very likely to become narrow well before Chippenham, and you would need to look at a longer term at your next shed." Henry spent a moment or two in thought and then replied, "Yes, sir. I will apply to Chippenham Shed. I cannot guarantee that I would pass the fireman's exam, although I would hope not to disgrace myself."

The shedmaster nodded. "I think that would be best," he said. "I might add that I will give you a good report; you have earned it here."

10 – Transfer to Chippenham (May 1872)

Henry was delighted to receive a positive reply to his letter from the Chippenham shedmaster; he was to report there at the beginning of the following week. On arrival at the shed, he was pleased to see his original belief confirmed: Chippenham was still purely broad gauge. He reported to Shedmaster Melrose in a cheerful frame of mind, but although the shedmaster expressed his pleasure at the report from his Oxford colleague, his news about accommodation was rather less welcome.

"As you can see, Cleaner Denton, this is an important junction, with a large shed staff; but Chippenham is not a large town like Oxford so finding accommodation is not easy. There is a cheap hotel not far away so you could book in there for a night or two and I'll see what I can do to find you somewhere suitable."

It was in fact three days before he was called into Mr Melrose's office to learn that accommodation for him had been found 'in a nearby farm'. After his shift, Henry immediately packed his bag and set off to the address he had been given, to discover that his and the shedmaster's idea of the meaning of the word 'nearby' differed considerably. The farm was three miles from the town so he had a daily walk of six miles to and from work.

It seemed that the ex-farm boy was going to be kept fit by both his walking as well as by any firing that he might be expected to do. But at twenty-three years of age this did not worry Henry unduly; he was much more interested in the work he would be doing.

Classified now as a Cleaner, he expected – and was given – plenty of work cleaning the locomotives and doing the sundry other jobs which were a cleaner's lot: cleaning engines, lighting up fires in fireboxes, filling the sandboxes with dry sand, fetching and carrying tools, and so on. The shedmaster wanted to know what the enginemen thought of Henry before he could make any real judgment.

Thus it was several weeks before Henry found himself assisting in the cab on a short freight to Calne. Driver Jeb Horncastle and his fireman Moses Hart were of course a perfectly competent cab crew but Assistant Shedmaster Bert Symonds wanted their opinion of Henry's ability to handle the firing shovel.

Driver Horncastle was a man of few words but Moses made up the shortfall by chattering constantly; a quirk which Driver Horncastle accepted without comment.

When Henry entered the cab, he found the fire already made up to requirement for the short run and Moses leaning at the back of the tender with a grin on his face.

"Now then, young Denton, Jeb here's going to drive this 'ere engine, an' I'm going to rest 'ere leanin' me arse on the toolbox just watchin' ye both. I'll say nuthin at all about yer firin' unless yer asks me. An' if'n yer ask me, I'll tell ye what ye want ter know, otherwise I'll keep me trap shut. If ye're cack 'anded, I'll tell Mr Symonds, an' if yer good at firin', I'll tell 'im that too."

Jeb Horncastle, watching this, nodded. "Aye, that's how it'll be."

Henry was pleased. This was exactly what he needed to get his hand in. For the next nine months, his unofficial use in firing duties increased as he gained in confidence. He learned the roads to Bristol, Salisbury and Didcot, some of the time acting as a fireman. He particularly enjoyed working with Fireman Hart and Driver Horncastle, who, he suspected, had been given the job of training him by Mr Melrose. After one especially heavy firing duty with the two of them, Moses Hart had remarked loudly enough on the cab to Jeb Horncastle, "I'll 'ave to watch meself, Jeb. If this 'ere lad keeps on like this, I might lose me job as yer reg'lar fireman!"

"Aye, Moses, yer might an' all," responded his driver.

Henry felt very flattered by this exchange, but the pleasure at his perceived progress at Chippenham Shed was dampened in late November after a heavy snowfall. He had accustomed himself to the six miles he had to walk every day and this augmented his already impressive physical fitness.

But the early snow had introduced a worrying aspect to his working routine. Mrs Wetherby, the farmer's wife, who looked after him very well, had warned him the winter snow up on the hill where the farm lay could get quite heavy on occasions and could even cut them off from the town. She suggested that he might try and find some digs nearer Chippenham. This disappointed him as he had been very happy with the Wetherbys, but he definitely needed to be able to get to work every day without fail.

Before he could do much about this, he was called into Shedmaster Melrose's office.

"Cleaner Denton, I have had several good reports about your duties here and I believe it is time for you to move up to Fireman status. As you have noticed, this shed is rather short of firemen. Have you prepared for the fireman's exam?"

Henry was both surprised and delighted to hear this, "Yes, Sir," he replied. He had indeed been studying the rules.

"Then you will make yourself ready for the formal and footplate examinations in two weeks' time. I will inform Paddington of your intention to apply."

"Thank you, sir." Henry left the shedmaster's office determined to study hard again and confirm his colleagues' faith in his abilities.

Some days later, he was called to Paddington, where the morning's questioning of the rules was followed by an hour's driving test under the aegis of a footplate inspector who, Henry thought, was happy with his performance but who made no comment, merely writing busily in his notepad.

It was another two weeks before Henry was called into the shedmaster's office. "Well? How do you think you went on your fireman's examination?"

"I'm unsure, sir," he replied. "I don't recall making any errors."

"No, young man, apparently you did not, according to Inspector Goldstein and Driver Pellew. They both gave you a good report. So as from last Tuesday, your wages have risen to three shillings and sixpence a week. Well done, Fireman Denton!"

"Thank you, sir!" Henry was delighted; he had finally become a formal locomotive footplateman. He determined to write to his parents to let them know the good news immediately. He might now, he realised suddenly, be able to afford to find somewhere closer to the town to live. He would sincerely regret leaving the Wetherbys; they had been very good to him and he had particularly enjoyed Mrs Wetherby's cooking.

His first duty as a fireman involved working a slow goods as far as Bristol, where it would be taken over by a Bristol & Exeter engine with a Taunton crew. He was very pleased to discover that he had been paired with Driver Jeb Horncastle.

"Don't think I'm goin' ter be easy on yer, young Henry," said Jeb with a grin. "Yer an official fireman now an' that means I don't 'ave ter coddle yer any longer."

Henry knew that Jeb wouldn't be unduly hard on him, but he was always careful in his firing; he remembered the bad mistake he had made in Oxford Yard, when he was with Driver Parkinson. He still had moments of shame when he thought about it.

They paused at Bathampton and Bath to do some shunting. After Henry had uncoupled the goods vans and wagons from their engine, a very plain-looking 0-6-0ST saddle tank Bristol & Exeter engine drew up to couple onto the train.

"It's got no name, Mr Horncastle," remarked Henry as watched its fireman couple up, "Just a number – 53."

"Ar, the B & E never put names on their injins like we do," said his driver. "We only do it on the narrer gauge ones, but I s'pose all our injins will 'ave numbers once the broad gauge goes. They might even 'ave names and numbers!" he smiled. "It'll keep them romantics in

Paddington thinkin'."

Just before they left Bristol to return to Oxford, Henry was astonished to see a huge 4-2-4T B &E tank engine No. 40 pulling in on a passenger train. It had the biggest single driving wheel he had ever seen.

"Ain't many o' them left," commented Jeb. "That big wheel is all o' nine-foot diameter!"

The return shift involved another slow goods to Oxford. They were to take it as far as Swindon, for an Oxford crew to take it on to its final destination. They paused to shunt once more at Bath and Bathampton again, and after Chippenham at Dauntsey and Wootton Basset, before handing over to the Oxford crew in Swindon Yard. Henry had been looking forward to this changeover; he was hoping he would know the Oxford men from his three years working there.

It was while shunting in the yard at Dauntsey that he thought once more of his Oxford accident. He wondered whether Driver Lawrence Parkinson would be the Oxford changeover driver and, if so, whether he would remember and tease Henry about his fall from grace.

He was thinking about a possible riposte when a sharp word "Henry!" from his driver brought him down to earth suddenly. He looked at Mr Horncastle, who pointed silently at the water gauges.

"Great heavens!" He had forgotten to check and the water level was low. He quickly turned the injector on, to bring the level up to what was required for their last few miles to Swindon.

Jeb Horncastle nodded as he saw the embarrassment on Henry's face; he knew that his fireman felt serious guilt about the lapse and decided that there was no reason to mention the matter further. He knew enough about Henry's character to know that Henry would see to it that such a slip would not happen again. As they pulled into Swindon Yard, Henry's face was still burning. A fine thing to occur on his first day as a fireman!

But as he saw the Oxford crewmen waiting for them, he had experienced very strange feelings; he recognised

Lawrence Parkinson with pleasure, mixed with apprehension about what he might say when he heard that the young cleaner he had known was now a fully-fledged fireman. He was not in suspense long.

"So it's Henry Denton, Great Western Fireman, we hear! Well done, young Henry. We always knew you had it in you." Driver Parkinson held out his hand to Henry's driver. "Larry Parkinson, I used to train this young cove when he was a cleaner at our shed. Very promising young feller he was, too. I'm so glad he's made the grade."

"Pleased ter meecher, I'm Jeb 'Orncastle. Yerse, 'e's bin a good lad an' deserves 'is new duties. I bin watchin' over 'im, too. It's 'is first day as a fireman an' 'e's done orlright, as I expected."

Driver Parkinson's fireman, however, took no part in the conversation; he climbed into the tender to start shovelling the coal forward, ignoring everyone else. Henry knew who the fireman was; he had known him as Driver Seth Burton, but Henry recalled the derailment near Maidenhead when Driver Burton had missed a signal. This had been one blot on his copybook too many and he had been demoted. Henry was saddened; he had liked Seth Burton.

"Is there much broad gauge work in Oxford, Mr Parkinson?" he asked.

"Broad gauge? Nah, it's nearly all narrer at Oxford now. The broad gauge tracks has all bin lifted t' the north, an' we don't see much south of Oxford neither, until ye get to Didcot. I know ye always did like the broad gauge engines."

Henry nodded sadly. He had got out just in time.

11 - The bullion train (1873)

Chippenham Shed was a rather different matter in comparison with Oxford; there was little standard gauge. Here, most of the railway business was conducted only on the broad gauge, to Henry's immense satisfaction. Yet all the West of England expresses were still broad gauge and there was little talk of changing such affairs in the immediate future. However, everyone knew (although this was rarely admitted) that sooner or later the axe would fall completely on Brunel's seven-foot system. In fact, it was to be another twenty years before the final closure.

Henry found himself very much at home in his new workplace, where he had once been before, on a transfer goods. Although the railway centre was smaller than Oxford, jointly with Westbury Shed to the south it supplied engines for the Salisbury line. One or two visiting drivers had mentioned Henry's growing reputation at Oxford Shed, and Chippenham enginemen were curious to see whether the new fireman was as competent as they had been led to believe. One thing he was very thankful for was that there was no need to deal with mixed gauge freights. He was firing entirely on the broad gauge out of Chippenham.

Nevertheless, proud reputation or no, Henry was at first restricted to short-distance freight duties, until he could prove himself a satisfactory fireman. Shedmaster Melrose was a man always prepared to listen to comments of others but invariably made up his own mind, based on his own observations. He was firm but fair and ran a tight shed. He was relaxed about the minor tricks of the younger members of the cleaning gangs and whenever a foreman brought a young fireman up before him on a misdemeanour, Melrose recalled his own young days. He was actually waiting for the day when a youngster was in front of him accused of doing something he himself hadn't done as a young fireman. So far, it hadn't happened.

After several months, Foreman Melrose had spoken to all the drivers that Henry had fired to and received positive reports. Indeed, two of them had asked the shedmaster for Henry as their regular fireman.

Jacob Hendy had told him, "He's a good lad, George. I know he's only a young fellow but he knows his stuff and I would even like him as my fireman if I didn't already have Martin Lancaster. With a bit more main line passenger experience, he'll be a fine addition to the top link crews."

Driver Hendy was a top link driver himself; one of the senior men crewing the most prestigious and important, mainly passenger, trains.

George Melrose nodded. "Yes, I met his Oxford shedmaster at a meeting in Paddington recently and he said much the same thing, Jake. I'll make a note of what you have told me and see what can be done. But just remember that I too have to stick to rules as well."

Jacob Hendy smiled, "The day you obey the rules, George we'll all get worried!"

"Out of my office, Driver Hendy!"

Jake walked out with a broad grin on his face. George Melrose was known throughout the division for having a mind of his own and an independent way of doing things. Jacob Hendy and George Melrose had been cleaners, firemen, and then drivers together, and were close friends. When an opportunity had arisen for promotion, Jacob had opted to stay on the footplate, whereas George had been persuaded by his own shedmaster to take the job at Chippenham. George had agreed and asked Jacob to transfer there as well.

The rather short mixed freight consisted of only seven vehicles, including a curious van of a type Henry had not seen before. Its doors were padlocked shut and there were no markings on it.

Driver Eli Kingston seemed happy with Henry's firing and had made no comment about the unusual van.

"There's a strange van in the train, Mister Kingston." Henry could not help mentioning it. "What is it?"

"It is a van, young Denton, that you don't talk about; not to anyone," replied his driver. "It's a bullion van and it's going to Plymouth, for the Navy to deal with. We take it to Bristol, where Bristol & Exeter men take over for the rest of the journey."

"Bullion? Like gold and silver?"

"Exactly, and it's also something else."

"What?"

"A target for evil-minded men, which is why we don't discuss it with anyone except railway officials."

Henry nodded; he could see that a broad gauge van could carry far more gold than a standard gauge could, and that was enough to tempt any gang.

They moved out of the yard and onto the main line to the west, before slowing down to come to a halt at the station platform, to wait for the starter signal that would allow them to proceed. Henry glanced at the gauges and into the firebox to check that all was ready. He had moved to the cabside to wait for the signal when he heard a low call from a top-hatted bystander on the platform.

"Yer've got a big injin there, lad, fer a short goods!"

This was quite true; their locomotive was a large 4-2-2 passenger locomotive called *Amazon*, of the Iron Duke class, and could certainly handle a short freight with ease. It was laughably overpowered for its seven vehicles. Henry had assumed that the engine was going back to another shed and that the GWR accountants rightly wanted to make sure it earned every penny possible.

Eli Kingston was over on the other side of the cab, filling and tamping his pipe.

"On a slow goods, are yer then?" the man on the platform asked.

"Looks like it," Henry replied offhandedly.

"Yer going through Bathampton?"

These were odd questions for man who was presumably waiting for his own train. What did it matter which route they took?

"I'm only the fireman; I do what my driver tells me,"

Henry responded. "I don't have to think about how or when we go anywhere."

Just then, the starter signal dropped and saved him from having to think of anything else to say without seeming rude. He saw the guard's green flag at the same time.

"We're clear to go, Mr K.," he called to the driver. "The guard's waved his flag."

"Right, then." The driver released the engine brake and began to ease his regulator up. The big engine moved off slowly. Driver Kingston asked, "Who were you talking to?"

"A passenger on the platform," Henry said disdainfully. "He was asking strange questions, like which our route was. He looked like a toff, but didn't speak like one."

"What do you mean?"

Henry paused. "I wonder," he said slowly, "whether he wasn't checking on our progress."

Eli Kingston thought for a moment and then nodded. "You could be right about that. You've a brain in your head, Henry."

They stopped in Bathampton and Driver Kingston went into the stationmaster's office, returning in a few minutes with three uniformed railway policemen. One of them, a sergeant, unlocked the bullion van and both he and the constables climbed in, locking the door again behind them.

"Those three peelers will give any evildoers a right nasty shock!" remarked Eli calmly as they moved off.

After entering Saltford Tunnel, they slowed right down.

"Sound the brake whistle to alert the guard, Henry!" called his driver. "When we come out of the tunnel, we could find an obstruction on the line!"

Sure enough, just outside the tunnel, a large log lay across the main down line, but Driver Kingston was able to stop the train before any damage could be done.

"Two short blasts on the whistle, Henry!" shouted Eli as he wound the brake on. Henry did as he was told then climbed down to set about removing the log from the track.

Four men; three with guns and the fourth with a sledgehammer, burst out of a small copse next to the line.

One jumped on the cab steps, threatening Henry's driver with his gun, while the man with the sledgehammer ran to the bullion van and smashed the padlock. Another threatened Henry, motioning him back into the cab, while the remaining man stood guard with his pistol.

The man with the sledgehammer slid the van door wide open. "Come on!" he shouted, turning to his mates, then began to climb in. Instantly, a shot rang out and he fell back onto the track, as the three armed police appeared at the door.

"Gor blimey!" yelled one of the men, watching the cab crew as he stared in shock. While the robbers were distracted, Henry grabbed a large lump of coal and hurled it at the head of the man on the cab steps, knocking him off the footplate, onto the track. The remaining two uninjured robbers took to their heels for the copse but were rapidly overtaken by the two constables, while the sergeant put a pair of handcuffs on the groaning man, who was lying on the track next to the locomotive and holding his head. The man with the hammer was clutching his leg as he writhed in agony on the ground.

The police sergeant smiled as he saw who it was. "I know that cove," he chuckled. "Thanks to you two enginemen, we've got this gang. They've bin giving us problems for some time now, but I doubt whether they'll provide any more. Armed robbery is a topping offence."

The thieves were loaded into the bullion van by the police, who locked the door behind them before joining the crewmen on the roomy footplate as Driver Kingston set the train in motion again.

There were no further incidents during the journey but there was a surprise for Henry at Bristol: the bullion van was detached and shunted into a siding, where a large horse-drawn van with barred windows was waiting. The door of the bullion van was opened and the four prisoners were herded out and loaded into the waiting prison van. The door was locked on the outside of the van and the three police climbed beside the driver, who flicked his reins at the two horses, who drew it off down the street. The locked bullion van was left on its own in the siding.

"The gold, Mr Kingston!" called Henry urgently when he saw that Eli was easing the brake off in preparation for moving back to couple up to the freight train once more. "There could be others in the gang who might take their chance. The gold is unguarded and the police have gone!"

Driver Kingston stopped what he was doing and reapplied the engine brake. "Come with me, Henry," he said climbing down from the cab.

Puzzled, Henry followed Eli back to the bullion van and watched while the driver took a large key from his pocket.

"The GWR police have been looking for that gang in the district for some time," Eli said as he slid the van door open. "Have a look inside, lad."

Henry did as he was told: apart from a bench, the van was completely empty.

12 - The Slough Slip (1873)

Henry was beginning to feel that he was finally becoming an experienced railwayman; it was now eleven years since he first joined the railway and he had practised most of the duties – even if only at a superficial level – of what was demanded of a Great Western fireman. Yet he was still in for a surprise. On a slow train from Paddington to the west one morning, he was waiting at Slough station when an express to Birmingham on the standard gauge track beside him hurried through. He paid no special attention until a few moments later a coach glided on the same track to a sedate stop at the platform.

"Look, Mr Kingston," he called to his driver, "the down Birmingham has parted and lost a coach on its way through! By a curious coincidence, it has stopped at the platform."

Driver Eli Kingston looked to see what had caught his fireman's attention. "Ah no, lad. The express has just slipped a coach for Slough; slipping a coach off the back of a train saves having to stop the whole train at the station. Passengers for Slough are informed at Paddington which coach to board before the train departs. Then just before Slough, at a special marker next to the track, a guard in the slip coach releases the coach and slows it so that it stops at the platform."

"But what if the passengers get into the wrong coach?"

Driver Kingston smiled, "They'll have to get off at Reading and catch a train back to Slough, and they'll know next time to follow instructions."

"Do we have other slips?"

"A few of the railway companies do it. The GWR finds it useful and are apparently thinking of extending the practice. I only know of slips for Slough and Banbury."

Although this practice required a special guard, the economy in not having to stop the whole train and then restart it again was enough to make the method of value, to say nothing of the benefit to timekeeping. In fact, the system was to continue for another eighty years.

Henry lodged a request to make a trip in a slip coach, to familiarise himself with the procedure. One morning, his request was granted. This unusual trip took place on a Paddington to Birmingham express. This time, he sat in the rear coach, to observe the slip guard's duty at Slough.

The guard needed to manipulate the release mechanism at the marker sign, in order to allow for the coach to glide to a stop at the platform. If the coach was slipped either too early or late, another engine would need to be called up to fetch it into the station and reprimands to all concerned would follow. The footplate crew also needed to know when the coach was slipped so that they did not assume that their train had parted. There was a special system of bells, by which means a large gong at the engine would sound.

On this trip, the slip guard, Silas Tompkins; a rather surly man with little to say for himself except to criticise his fellow men, told Henry to simply watch, and keep his mouth shut. About half an hour out of Slough, he told Henry to go and check the passengers, to ascertain that they all had tickets for Slough and to warn them that if not they would have to leave and rebook at Reading, at their own extra expense.

Henry did as he was bid and was moving along the corridor back to his place next to the guard at the front window when he was stopped by a charming and rather attractive young lady.

"Pray tell me, sir," she smiled at him sweetly, "when does this train stop in Slough?"

Henry was captivated and a sense of mischief asserted itself. "Slough, madam? I regret to inform you that it does not." Henry watched the delightful smile disappear, to be replaced by a pout of annoyance.

"Oh, that is distressing. I was sure that I had caught the correct train at Paddington. I do not understand how I came to commit such an error!"

Henry knew of course that the young lady had not made an error; although the train was not scheduled to stop there, the slip coach was, and there would have been an announcement to that effect at Paddington. She had either not heard or had forgotten this.

Henry was about to correct her and explain when he had a sudden idea; she was almost certainly unaware of the slip coach arrangement and he could impress her mightily if she thought he had stopped the train just for her.

"Oh, finding the right train at Paddington can be so confusing for a young and – permit me to say this – attractive lady," he stated gallantly.

She blushed, "Oh, sir, you are too kind."

"I think I might be able to stop the train at Slough for you," he said slowly, waiting for her reaction.

The girl's blue eyes widened in admiration. "Oh, that would be wonderful. I cannot think why I boarded the wrong train, sir."

Henry smiled at her. "I cannot make any promises, but I will endeavour to do my best. Let us see whether we can be in Slough in less than fifteen minutes."

"I would be so grateful." Now her eyes were downcast and Henry hoped this was very promising and could perhaps even lead to a possible later meeting. But no, he would not think any further; that would be simply too good to be true. Nevertheless, he was determined to convince the young lady that he was an influential member of the GWR staff. One should always exploit one's opportunities.

He left the young lady sitting expectantly in her seat and walked through to the guard's compartment, to watch Silas Tompkins prepare to release the coach. Guard Tompkins was watching diligently out of the window for the marker point at which he should detach. Reaching the aforesaid point, he undid the locking mechanism and reached for the lever to uncouple the coach from the train, which was now travelling at a requisite speed to facilitate the release.

But there appeared to be a problem. The guard was struggling with the lever and Henry heard his muttered imprecations.

"Don't just stand there, you buffoon, give me a hand here!" he snarled at Henry.

Henry reached over to help but caught his hand in the mechanism. It took another half-minute to finally release the coach, which was now still travelling at a considerable speed, while the rear of the rest of their train was gradually distancing itself. The slip coach rolled along smoothly, with the guard frantically turning the brake, but unfortunately it was still not slow enough and the coach glided gently through the platform at Slough Station, coming to a halt 200 yards clear of the platform.

As Henry hurried back to the station, dispatched by the guard to explain the failure of the release mechanism, the station pilot engine moved out along their track to retrieve the coach and draw it back into the platform. While the relieved passengers disembarked, Henry and the guard were called into an office to explain why Guard Tompkins had allowed the coach to overrun the platform. Silas Tompkins took an inspector back into the coach to show the faulty release hook and Henry corroborated the guard's explanation as the official noted down all the details.

Back in the office, before he caught an up train back to Paddington, Guard Tompkins surprised Henry by thanking him for his support.

Henry now had an hour's wait until he could return to Chippenham on the next down train and so went onto the platform to see if the young lady was still about.

She was sitting on a bench on the platform, talking to a young fellow who by his dress Henry judged to be a farm worker. The young fellow wasn't happy about something, Henry observed, but the young lady appeared adamant. The farm worker shook his head and stalked off.

The girl looked up to see Henry standing there. "Oh," she said, smiling, "it's the young railwayman who stopped the train for me. How very nice to see you again!"

"It was really no trouble, madam," replied Henry. "I was happy to be able to assist."

The young lady looked him up and down, then stood up.

"Come with me," she murmured quietly.

Henry followed her as she walked to a small shed on the platform. This shed was for the permanent way men to store some of their tools. The girl paused and looked around; nobody was watching so she indicated that they should enter. It was cramped and dusty inside, with tools neatly stacked

The girl backed against a wall. "Give me a kiss!" she whispered.

A delighted Henry lurched forward and held her waist while she kissed him firmly several times. He could hardly believe his luck! But while he was briefly aware of her hands on his waist, he paid little attention to them until his trousers slipped down. Startled, he bent to retrieve them, but she stopped him and lifted her dress high above her knees to display, to Henry's dumbfounded eyes, a pair of white thighs, unimpeded by any bloomers.

"We must be quick," she whispered, "before anyone comes in."

Before he could react, she had seized him, and he shut his eyes helplessly at her manipulations.

Some minutes later, the red-faced and shaken young fireman listened silently as the girl said firmly, "I shall leave first, and you will adjust your attire before leaving the hut, but kindly wait a few moments and do not appear to follow me out!" She left and strolled along the platform.

Henry, having obediently waited five minutes, left in time to see her disappear through the station exit.

He felt both highly embarrassed and ashamed; she was clearly a girl of easy virtue and, although she was far prettier, she nevertheless reminded him of Clerk Ambrose Bolton's daughter in Oxford Shed, offering rapid relief to randy enginemen at sixpence a time. Henry's beliefs about females had received a sudden correction to those he had formed in his hitherto sheltered existence.

He caught the next down train to Chippenham feeling miserable and totally disgusted with himself, especially as he had felt so disappointed at his Oxford colleagues. He tried to forget the experience by devoting himself wholeheartedly to his duties. This was not the kind of start to his life at the new shed that he had envisaged for himself and it was many months before he could forget the shame of his reaction to the thrill of seduction by a beautiful girl's urging in Slough.

He had of course already written to his parents to inform them of his promotion to fireman and had received a reply expressing their pride and congratulations. He had kept in fairly regular contact but hadn't actually visited them for several years, and his sense of family concern finally persuaded him to arrange some leave, in order to see for himself how they were and how the farm was prospering.

Now that he was officially a fireman, he was entitled to a reduction in his travel fares on the GWR. It was a whole week before he realised that these considerations helped to take his mind off his despicable fall from grace in Slough.

13 – A ride on the 'Narrow' again (March 1879)

Henry was looking forward to seeing his parents, who had sold the family farm to Elijah Wingate. Eli had been of invaluable assistance at the farm, especially after Henry had left, and had subsequently made Mr and Mrs Denton an acceptable offer for the property.

Henry's parents had moved into a small house in Upton-by-Chester, quite close to the main Chester-Birkenhead railway line. Upton even had its own little station so that they did not need a pony and trap to visit the shops in the city. They could also take a day trip to Birkenhead or Liverpool if they crossed the Mersey on the big, modern ferry at the brand-new Woodside Station.

Woodside had been completed the previous year, to replace the older Monks Ferry Station for passengers on the ferry to Liverpool. Mr and Mrs Denton already knew from Henry's letters that he had been promoted to fireman and Mr Denton had contacted a local railwayman he knew who had told him that this, at the age of twenty-three, was a real feather in Henry's cap. His parents were so pleased that they fully forgave him his abandonment of the family farm. Henry only wished he could bring them further news of a young lady of interest but the embarrassment he still felt at his meeting with the young lady in Slough, in addition to his need to walk the long distance to and from work, had precluded most social activities.

He took a Paddington express as far as Didcot, where he intended to change into a narrow gauge Birkenhead express. On the platform, he waited with other passengers and watched as a broad gauge down goods on the mixed gauge track to the west passed through the station.

"Why is it going so slowly, Father?" asked a small boy.

The father shook his head. "I don't know, Peter. It's a mystery to me."

Henry smiled and walked over to the pair. "If you look carefully," he said, "you'll see that on mixed gauge track, the narrow gauge always veers to the platform side as it passes through a station."

The boy's father gazed at Henry in surprise. "How do you know all that? Are you a railwayman?"

"That's right," replied Henry. "I'm a Great Western fireman."

"But why does the narrow gauge come to the platform side... ? Oh, I see, of course!" The man suddenly realised. "It's because with passenger trains the passengers have to disembark safely."

"Yes," said Henry. "That's right."

"But why do goods trains run so slowly here?"

"All trains need to slow down," explained Henry. "That is so that there is less strain on the couplings as they pass through the stations, otherwise they might get wrenched as the standard gauge track moves to the platform side."

Henry recalled when his driver once had to do that on a goods from Oxford to South Wales when he was firing some years back. His driver had told him to keep a sharp eye out on the wagons as they passed through the stations. This was an aspect of the broad gauge he had completely forgotten.

"Then I think it's really time this broad gauge was abandoned," remarked the father. "It causes too many problems."

Henry's Birkenhead express arrived and he boarded it, eager to see how smoothly it ran. He was interested to discover whether the standard gauge track matched the quality of Brunel's broad gauge concept, which had earlier shown superiority over most of the standard gauge rails laid by northern engineers. Over the next three hours, he found that the original superiority of Brunel's broad gauge track design had apparently disappeared. Poor maintenance of track which should have been replaced, plus the improvement in standard gauge track, had resulted in little appreciable difference in the two systems; if anything, the permanent way standards and tracklayers' skills had more than caught up with the original broad gauge designs. By now, the only advantage of the broad gauge trains existed in memory alone.

The GWR main broad gauge route to the West Country was still extremely popular with passengers and its conversion to standard gauge was thought to be some years away yet. Nevertheless, Henry looked forward to this run on a standard gauge train for the five or so hours needed to reach his home town. He had even thought of trying to catch the London & North Western's crack Irish Mail express, but to do that he would have had to pay the extra fare to London and then book onto a North Wales train from Euston, to run via Chester. Loyalty to his own company (aside from the fare discount for company employees) convinced him to use the slightly longer GWR route.

Henry's parents were predictably delighted to see their son again and rejoiced in his elevated status at the GWR. He had to answer many questions about his duties. It was clear to both parents that their son was happy in his job, which softened their disappointment about handing the farm out of the family.

"Now, Henry," began his mother in the firm tone he knew so well, "it's time you took more care of your appearance. I will take you into the city tomorrow and we can look for better clothes for you. I'm sure you haven't bought anything respectable for many years." She viewed his clothing with a mother's eye. "One day you will be wanting a promotion to Driver and you must be able to look the part." Henry knew better than to argue; in any case, he wanted to see what the city looked like. As a boy, he hadn't known it well because they had lived in the country and rarely visited the city centre itself.

Walking through Eastgate Street, with its multitude of shops and now famous rows, he was surprised to see rails along the centre of the street. "What's going on here?" he asked.

"Oh that," replied his mother. "We've got trams running everywhere in town. I don't know why; surely our omnibuses can do the job more cheaply. It's my view that the corporation simply wants to show that it's a modern thinking body. Other cities are apparently doing the same thing." The rails continued further down Bridge Street and swung right towards the castle, where they finished.

Henry saw one of the new trams, with its horse moving slowly along. "They're talking of extending the trams as far out as Saltney," remarked his mother as they stopped to watch.

Three days later, on his return, Henry's train came to an unscheduled stop just north of Shrewsbury, on a stretch of track he knew well. Looking out of his window, Henry stared in horror. He saw a scene of smashed carriages, people being laid out alongside the track, and in the distance smoke curling up from the chimney of a locomotive that was right off the track and leaning precariously. Henry climbed down and hurried along to the accident, to see whether he could help.

A burly policeman stopped him angrily. "We don't need starin' bloody sightseers! Bugger off!"

"I'm a Great Western fireman returning to duty. I might be able to help," explained Henry.

"Oh aye, yer might at that. Very well, go on an' tell my colleague over yonder I sent yer through."

Henry hurried on past what had been a very long excursion train, judging by the carriages. They were predominantly old four-wheelers and, Henry suspected, should have been condemned years ago. Most companies kept their old stock for just such occasions. He counted twenty-five coaches, the first four of which had been thrown right off the track. The first coach was lying on its side and had apparently pulled the tender of the train engine off with it when it derailed. The pilot engine was quietly simmering, still coupled to the train engine.

"What can I do to help?" Henry asked a railway official, who seemed to be giving a variety of instructions.

"And you are?" enquired the official, looking him up and down carefully.

"I'm Fireman Denton from Chippenham Shed, sir, returning from a three-day leave."

"Ah, yes, then. You might be very useful. Have a look at the first carriage and see if you can find what brought it off the road."

There were four bodies covered over and a much larger number of passengers sitting silently, waiting to be taken to the nearest medical attention. Henry walked back to the coach to see what might have caused the derailment. The side of the carriage was badly shattered but Henry was more interested in the track. One of the rails had been slewed several inches to one side but didn't seem to show any obvious flaws. He checked the coach's wheels. One of them was smaller in diameter than the other three, and missing a flange.

He hurried back to the official. "I think a tyre came off one of the coach's wheels, sir."

The official groaned. "I might've known. They always use this old stock for their excursions and they so often cause us problems. By the way, I'm Inspector Reece from Salop, and thank you, young man. I'll see to it that your shedmaster hears of your valuable assistance. Chippenham, you said?"

Henry nodded.

They returned to the first coach and he crawled underneath. "I've got it, sir!" he called out dragging the broken tyre behind him.

They both examined it.

"See, sir, there's the crack." Henry pointed to where the tyre had cracked and opened out and loosened itself from the wheel.

"That's one of the main reasons why they should scrap these old coaches," grunted Inspector Reece. "The iron was of poor quality, leading to flaws in the forged tyre." It was to be another five hours before the track was cleared and Henry could continue his journey back to Chippenham.

His way back south was full of memories: Wolverhampton was a familiar sight but there was no longer any sign at all of the original broad gauge there. At Oxford, too, he only glimpsed a short length of the broad gauge track on a disused siding. He left the train at Didcot to catch a down Bristol express as far as Chippenham.

His landlady was keen to hear all about his visit to such a distant place as Chester. She, like most people in the country, had rarely travelled more than about twenty miles from her home, although the advent of the railways was beginning to make more distant travel a much more common affair than would have been imaginable fifty years earlier. She was a motherly type and took a keen interest in the young fireman's life, wondering whether it wasn't time for him to think about 'walking out' (as she put it to herself) with a nice young lady. So far, he had shown no such inclination, stating that his duties precluded any serious social life.

Henry set to educate himself about firing on a range of different engines, so that he could observe how different drivers handled their locomotives. He offered to assist on any unpopular firing duties, arguing to himself that the range of experiences would stand him in good stead for any future promotion prospects.

One morning, he was listed to fire a local passenger to Salisbury via Westbury with Driver Brian Wisdom, known to all as 'Brainy'. Henry could understand this from Driver Wisdom's name but his actions did not match his nickname at all. He was friendly enough on the run south but his poor memory was a constant surprise to Henry.

The driver tried to climb on a broad gauge engine, completely forgetting that the track to Salisbury had already been converted to standard gauge.

When Henry had pointed out the error, Brainy merely shrugged and said, "Oh aye, o' course. Anyone can make a mistake."

Yet his driving technique, if Henry was any judge, was perfectly competent.

On their return, they had a lengthy signal stop at Westbury and Henry was impressed with what he could see

of the railway setup there.
   This seems to be a good place to work, he thought to himself, even though the broad gauge is losing out.

14 - "Good job it were broad gauge!" (September 1881)

Henry Denton had been working as a fireman now for two years and was enjoying his life with the GWR. Nothing was perfect, of course; for example, he had the onerous duty of firing for the shed bully, Driver Leonard Hartford. Driver Hartford worked his firemen very hard and seemed to relish being able to make their lives a misery whenever an opportunity arose. Thanks to Driver Hartford, Henry had discovered the truth of the proverb 'No gain without pain'. He certainly gained experience with this competent driver but acquiring the expertise could be painful.

One of the driver's favourite tricks was driving slowly near the end of a shift, when he could see his fireman was weary. Then he would pull his watch from his waistcoat, examine it, and call out, "Deary me, Henry, we're running late! We'll have to get cracking!" Followed by a sudden lifting of the regulator, leading to a violent draught that would tear great holes in Henry's carefully tended fire. Driver Hartford would then glance into the firebox and growl, "Come on, boy, get that fire going properly, you're supposed to be a real fireman now!"

Henry would have to shovel hard and carefully to repair the damage just when he had been hoping for an easy run home. Most of his firing colleagues felt the same way about 'Heavy Hartford', as he was known.

But today his driver was Graham Dunwich, who was both friendly and skilful. Firing to him was illuminating and entertaining. He had a large fund of railway experiences, with which he would regale his fireman. These experiences were usually helpful illustrations of what to do in a variety of situations. In addition, they had *Fowler*, an 0-6-0T of the Sir Watkin class of goods tank locomotives. This engine was fitted with not only a part roof but a high spectacle plate as well; it had just come out of a routine maintenance at Swindon and was running sweetly. Their train was an eastbound goods from Bristol to Acton yard, and the autumn weather was glorious. All was right with the world.

Yet both men were about to add a unique experience to their lives. As they were nearing Slough, they approached a small wooded area, out of which burst a young runner, carrying a bag and hurrying across the field next to the line. At intervals, he stuck a hand into the bag and tossed out some scraps of paper.

"A hare from Eton College," remarked Driver Dunwich as they watched with interest. A sudden shout echoed as a bunch of lads raced out of the wood and caught sight of their 'hare'.

"They'll have him now!" called Henry, grinning. "He can't get away from them." But the hare, hearing the shout, glanced behind and put a spurt on, racing parallel to the track. He must have decided to dodge across to the other side and he leapt over the fence and ran directly across the path of the train, even though Driver Dunwich whistled frantically. The lad tripped and fell headlong between the longitudinal baulks between the rails. Before he could get up, the engine had passed right over him. The driver applied the emergency brake and the train screeched to a stop.

Both crewmen climbed down from the cab, one at each side, and walked to where they anticipated a dreadful sight. They peered apprehensively between the wheels of a wagon, where they could see the body. They both started in shock when it moved slowly and tried to rise, bumping its head on an axle.

"What on earth?" said the young lad, rubbing his head. "What happened?"

He slowly scrambled out from under the wagon, to find himself being hauled up to stare at Driver Dunwich. "Who are you, sir?" he shook his head, clearly dazed.

"I'm the engine driver who has just run you down, young shaver," replied Driver Dunwich grimly. "You tried to cross the track right in front of our train."

"Ran me down?"

"Aye, lad, you were the hare and the hounds nearly had you, so you dodged across the railway just as we were coming past. You tripped and fell between the rails, then hit your head when you got up."

By this time, the rest of the pack had arrived. They were shocked at what had happened, although very relieved to see their friend alive and standing up. Driver Dunwich told them to go straight back to the college and report the incident to the headmaster there.

He, meanwhile, would take the hare to Slough Station under the stern supervision of the guard, and hand him over to the railway authorities for medical attention and so that the crew could report the incident. The boy would be looked after and returned to the college.

At Slough, both driver and fireman were taken off their duty and a Slough crew took the train on to its destination, while Driver Dunwich and Fireman Denton entered the details of the incident into their report.

"That lad's also the luckiest young man in Britain for another reason," remarked Graham Dunwich as they waited for their return shift back to Chippenham.

"What other reason?" Henry queried. "What do you mean?"

"He's lucky that he goes to Eton," said Graham, grinning.

"Why?"

"If he'd gone to Harrow, up north of London and been run over, he'd now be in several pieces. The North Western is standard gauge, with rails less than five foot apart. He's taller than that!"

On their return working, they were to take a goods from Acton to Bristol as far as Swindon, where a Bristol crew would take over. They expected to be told to catch a local passenger train and travel 'on the cushions' back to Chippenham to sign off duty.

This time their engine was *Humber*, an 0-6-0 goods engine

no longer in peak condition. Most of the other engines in its class had already been scrapped. It was a struggle to keep it running. They paused in Reading Yard to add two more vans to the load and fortunately were able to drop three at Didcot before trundling slowly along to Swindon Yard. Here, an inspector was waiting as they pulled up in the arrival siding.

"Sorry, Driver, I must ask you to take your train into the departure sidings yourself. The relief crew are late and haven't arrived here yet. I'll let Chippenham know why you're late."

Graham Dunwich nodded. "Fine, sir, we'll do that. And thank you." The inspector walked away and Driver Dunwich moved the train slowly across the points towards the departure siding. As he did so, a railway clerk from the neighbouring works appeared, engrossed in reading a newspaper, and strode across the tracks in front of them.

"Look out, you foozling idiot!" yelled Graham furiously, but he was too late. The engine nudged the clerk, who fell down between the rails. Driver Dunwich brought the train to a jerking stand as Henry jumped off and tried to see where the victim was lying. His mind was again full of expected horrors but the clerk crawled out from under one of the vans and stood up furiously. "Why in the name of all that's holy didn't your fool driver sound his whistle?" he shouted at Henry.

Graham Dunwich, shaking with rage, came up with his fists ready to commit murder but Henry grabbed his shoulder and held him back. The inspector had heard the shouting and the squealing of the brakes and came to see what had happened.

The clerk saw him and was instantly relieved. "Thank goodness you're here, Mr Clapton. This driver here has just knocked me over with his engine and, adding insult to injury, made a serious verbal attack on me!"

Inspector Clapton took a notebook out of his pocket, stating to the clerk, "That is a serious allegation, Clerk Needham. I shall have to note the details."

"Indeed, sir."

The inspector turned to Driver Dunwich. "I would like your name, Driver."

"Driver Dunwich, sir. Chippenham Shed."

"Thank you. Now, Needham here has alleged that you ran him down and insulted him. Is that correct?"

"Not entirely, sir, although we did run him down. He walked across the track reading a newspaper, right in front of us. We shouted but he didn't seem to hear us."

"And the insult?"

"There was no insult, sir."

"The man's lying, Mr Clapton! He did insult me!"

Inspector Clapton looked at Henry. "And you are Driver Dunwich's fireman, I take it?"

"Yessir. Fireman Denton, also of Chippenham."

"Fireman Denton, can you explain why this clerk was run over?"

"Yes, sir. You told us to move the train to the departure siding. We were just doing that when Clerk - er - Needham walked across the track. There was no time to do anything but shout a warning."

"And what did Driver Dunwich shout?"

"He called on Mr Needham to watch out, sir."

Graham Dunwich interrupted Henry. "I called him a foozling idiot, sir."

"There you have it, Mr Clapton, sir!" Clerk Needham called out triumphantly. "The man admits it himself!"

"And that's not an insult?" asked the inspector.

"No, sir, not under the circumstances."

"What?" Clerk Needham couldn't believe his ears. "Not an insult?"

Inspector Clapton raised his eyebrows in a questioning glance at Driver Dunwich.

"What would you call a railwayman, sir," Graham Dunwich asked, "who walks across a track reading a newspaper, without checking that the track has no approaching train on it?"

"He's changing the subject, sir. He's trying to deny the insult!" interrupted Clerk Needham indignantly.

Graham stared at the clerk. "Nonsense!" he said,

"'Foozling idiot' is not an insult: it's a description – and an accurate one at that!"

The inspector noted something in his little book and then addressed the clerk. "I'm very much afraid that Driver Dunwich is quite correct, Clerk Needham. A railwayman who does what you did really is an idiot." He shut his book, adding, "You may wish to take the matter further with your own department, but if I am called to witness – and I am certain I would be – you know now what I would say." He snapped his notebook shut. "Now, I have further duties to undertake. Good day to you all."

Clerk Needham stormed off in a rage but Henry, glancing back as they left, heard the inspector chuckling as he returned to his duties. Henry and his driver walked back from the yard to Swindon Station to catch a local passenger back to Chippenham Shed, where they related their adventures to their amused colleagues in the enginemen's cabin.

Fireman Arthur Smith commented, "Did you two realise, you've broken a record?"

"Record?" queried Graham Dunwich. He looked at Henry, "What's Arthur talking about?"

"I don't know."

"Yerse," continued Arthur. "You've run over two coves in only one trip and killed neither of 'em!"

There was a roar of laughter at the remark.

They left the cabin, passing the oldest driver, Willy Branson, who shook his head as he remarked, "Good job it were broad gauge you was workin' on!"

15 - An affair of the heart (1882)

On his return to Chippenham from a local to Bristol, Henry passed a young lady waiting on a bench on the down platform, accompanied by her little dog. As he walked past, the dog jumped out at him and nipped his ankle.

"Oh goodness me, I am so sorry!" gasped the young lady, tugging the errant pooch back on his lead towards her feet. "Are you hurt?"

Henry shook his head "No, miss," he said, "I'm wearing boots and your dog's teeth didn't get through the leather."

"Nevertheless, I must make amends. May I buy you a cup of tea in the cafeteria here?"

Henry thought for a moment and decided that he was thirsty and that a cup of tea with a young lady (who was in fact quite personable) would be welcome, and he nodded his agreement. In the ensuing conversation in the cafeteria, it transpired that Martha was a local girl who worked in service for a wealthy family in the town.

They chatted easily for twenty minutes before Henry remembered that he had to get back to the shed to book off-duty. He stood to apologise for departing and the girl seemed rather disappointed.

"Do you have to leave so soon?" she asked. "I was enjoying our little chat."

"I am really sorry, Martha," he said, realising that he meant what he said, "but I have to go. Perhaps we could meet on my day off sometime?"

"Oh yes, I would like that."

They arranged to have tea together the following Sunday afternoon when both, fortuitously, had the day off. On his long walk back, it occurred to Henry that he was looking forward to meeting with Martha again, yet the suspicion grew in his mind that he was doing exactly what he had decided not to; succumbing to the temptation of meeting a female. Over the next couple of days, he wrestled with the thought that he should simply not show up at the tea shop; but no, he told himself, that would be cowardly. He would have tea, chat for twenty minutes or so, and then leave without making any further arrangements. That would solve his problem.

The meeting did not go as planned: they chatted for far longer than Henry had intended and when he paid the bill and they left the tea shop, before he remembered his earlier resolve Henry had suggested another meeting. Martha's instant assent allayed his fears; he had by this time convinced himself that she was not the sort of girl who would exploit an unwary man.

He wasn't aware of it at the time but in Martha, Henry, like a fortunate leprechaun, had just found a pot of gold at the end of a rainbow.

They met on irregular occasions, whenever they could, over the next few months, until one day Martha told Henry that she had joined a choir and asked whether he too would be interested in joining it. Henry was caught by surprise: singing was emphatically not an interest of his but the girl equally emphatically was. He agreed so that he could see her at least once every month.

Henry found the choral sessions something of a trial but he persisted until gradually Martha herself lost interest. By the time she had, their monthly meetings had become weekly, and more important for both. It was now understood that they were formally 'walking out' together.

But Martha wasn't the only reason for Henry's growing elation. Shedmaster Melrose at Chippenham had recommended him to take his driver's exam. Three days later, with a pleased smile on his face, he called Henry into his office to inform him that he had passed and was now a qualified driver, with the wage to match.

"Now, Driver Denton, I will expect great things of you, but of course you understand that you will start your duties on the lowest shunting link."

"Yes, sir."

"I do not anticipate that you will stay too long on that link, of course."

"I will do my best, sir."

"I would not expect anything else."

"Thank you, sir."

Henry was jubilant that he had finally achieved his greatest ambition; he was determined to show that his chief's faith in him was not misplaced. That evening, he wrote a letter to his parents, giving them his good news. He posted it before hurrying to a meeting with Martha. She too, would be so pleased to hear of his success, he thought. Their choral sessions had now been abandoned entirely (to Henry's relief) and they were free to spend the evening together.

He arrived early at work the following morning and read the notices to check his duty. His engine for the day's shunting was *Regulus* of the Caesar class, an 0-6-0 goods engine with Jackie Cornwell as his fireman. He climbed on his engine and immediately began to check the fire, taking the coal hammer to some of the coal, when a shout stopped him.

"Now, now, Mr Denton, that's my job!" Jackie climbed into the cab and gently took the hammer from him. "You drive her, I fire her!"

Henry grinned in embarrassment. "So you do, Jackie. I'm sorry, I forgot myself for a moment." He moved over the wide space to the driver's side of the cab and began to check the steam and brake gauges; the engine had already been prepared by another crew. They spent the morning shunting, had their lunch on the ground next to their engine, then climbed aboard again for the afternoon shift.

This was an easy first day's driving for Henry. He was more fortunate than he realised in this day's work; he had been given this particular engine by Mr Melrose, who knew that it was still in fair condition and suitable for shunting. The Ariadne class engines were old and had by now mostly been scrapped or otherwise disposed of. Indeed, even the Caesar class *Regulus* herself was only to last another couple of years.

The shedmaster, having surreptitiously kept an eye on the work of his latest driver, nodded to himself, satisfied that the man knew his job. He would soon move him into the reserve link, used for the odd duties which cropped up from time to time in any busy yard: replacing absent drivers in shunting turns, shed piloting, or taking local goods or passenger trains.

Curiously, Henry's first stint at driving a passenger train occurred two months later on the standard gauge, as he was listed to take one from Chippenham to Westbury, where a Yeovil crew would take the train on to Weymouth. He would return on a goods to Swindon and come home from there 'on the cushions'. Nothing much in the way of long-distance work but a testing duty nevertheless, thought the shedmaster.

Henry was paired once more with Fireman Cornwell and the short run to Westbury was uneventful. They had over ninety minutes' break there, and Henry took the opportunity to have a good look around the station and yard. This area had already been converted to narrow - he must get used to calling it 'standard' gauge, he told himself - as by now the majority of the Great Western was either mixed gauge or 'Stephenson's standard', as some knew it. Broad gauge routes were being converted at a rapid pace, and new locomotives from Swindon were planned for the standard gauge, although it was expected that the main line to the west would require more broad gauge engines before it was converted. They could, it was decided, be built as 'convertibles': broad gauge engines which would have the usual inside frames, cylinders and motion but would be fitted with broad gauge wheels, to be replaced when required.

Westbury itself, Henry considered, was an interesting place, even though there was little evidence left of the broad gauge which once dominated the area. Although the town was relatively small, he liked the look of it in the half-hour or so that they had to look around.

Their return goods arrived and they took over from the Yeovil crew. The locomotive was one of the newer

Armstrong Goods 0-6-0 engines, designed to be a goods engine. Although it was standard gauge, Henry was impressed with its running. The engine ran sweetly over the re-laid track and its lengthy freight load caused it no problems whatsoever. Even the cab, relatively narrow compared to those Henry was used to, gave plenty of protection to its crew; it even had a roof to keep the worst of the weather off, and he enjoyed the return run as far as Swindon.

"What do you think, Jackie?" he asked his fireman.

"She's a fine engine, Mr Denton," replied Jackie Cornwell. "She's coping with the load and she's easy to fire. I like this engine."

Henry nodded in agreement, "Yes, she'll do."

In Chippenham, however, his mind was distracted by a very different matter: Martha had been dismissed from her position. The father of the family which had employed her as a nanny had been secretly running up serious gambling debts and the family had been obliged to cut its expenditure and move to cheaper accommodation. They could no longer afford to employ a nanny.

Henry saw his chance and, quite out of character, decided to act quickly. He proposed to Martha, knowing that with an increased wage he could support a wife and – intriguing thought – even a family. Martha instantly accepted; she had long ago decided that she would be a very suitable wife for him and had been waiting for Henry to realise this.

Martha's parents were delighted to see their daughter happy and raised no objection. The quiet wedding took place and the happy couple moved into a small flat until they could decide where they wanted to settle.

On his next free day, Henry took Martha to Westbury, to see what she thought of the town. He was already climbing up the links in Chippenham Shed but was thinking of moving when the broad gauge finally closed. Westbury had been on his mind.

Martha, meanwhile, found that her life was radically changed; she was now a married woman and had to get used to having a husband who needed feeding at very strange hours. Enginemen normally had shift work at irregular times. Henry would often be called out at three or four in the morning, with a knock at the door by the shed's young 'knocker up', whose job was to go round to the homes of shed staff and wake them for their shifts.

Little Herbie, Chippenham's 'knocker up', was a small but determined young lad of thirteen years, who was perfectly capable of ignoring bad language from the men he woke. He would throw stones at the window until the engineman actually got dressed and came out threatening murder. By then, there was then little chance of the man climbing back into a warm bed.

Once back in the shed, Herbie was safely under the protection of the shedmaster, who much appreciated Herbie's ability to get the men out on time to work on time.

Jackie Cornwell had arrived on shed and was preparing the fire on his engine when he heard running footsteps. He looked out to see young Herbie hurtling past with 'Thump' Marshall, the shed's bully fireman, striding after him.

"Wait till I catch ye, ye little turd!" Thump shouted. "Broke me bloody winder, 'e did," he said, seeing Jackie staring. Thump was known to be lazy as well as free with his fists.

Hearing the ruckus, Mr Melrose came out of his office just as Herbie was passing.

"Anything wrong here, Fireman Marshall?" he called.

Thump shuddered to a sudden stop. "Oh – er, no, sir. Just 'avin' a bit o' fun, sir."

"Well, perhaps you'd like to have more fun preparing your engine; you're ten minutes late on duty again. Once more and you'll be fined!"

With his new married status and increasing responsibilities as a driver on the GWR, Henry's satisfaction with his life grew immeasurably, but without his being aware of it, his captivation for everything broad gauge was gradually diminishing. The type of gauge he was working was becoming less of a concern to him. Driving trains was his forte and whether broad or narrow, the duty was much the same on both.

16 - Lord Willoughby's journey
(March 1888)

"Sorry, Driver Denton." The platform inspector came over as they paused in Reading station with the morning 11.40 from Paddington to the west. "You're to have an extra saloon added to the rear of the train. You may have to try and make up the time; we weren't expecting this addition."

"Shouldn't take too long, surely?" remarked Henry, as he quickly checked the steam pressure and glanced into the fire hole. "I'm sure we can catch up the extra few minutes between here and Bristol."

The inspector smiled briefly. "I hope so," he said slowly.

"You sound uncertain, sir." Henry looked at him carefully. "Is there something about this extra coach we should know?"

"It's a private saloon, Driver Denton, hired by Lord Willoughby, who is an influential shareholder in the company. He can be, erm – a little, er – demanding at times."

"But surely that won't affect us. He'll stay in his coach, won't he?"

"I hope so, for your sake," replied the inspector and moved off along the platform to his office.

"There's something odd here, Caleb," Henry turned to his fireman. "That inspector moved away too quickly for my liking. He's not telling us everything about this cove...?"

"You there! Driver!" A loud and impatient-sounding call came from the platform.

Henry moved to the side of the cab and looked down to see a small man with a large moustache and wearing a top hat.

"Yes, sir? What can I do for you?"

"I understand you are to take me to Wootton Bassett this morning."

"Certainly sir, if you are a passenger on this train."

"I'll have you know, Driver, that I am not 'sir', I am 'my lord'."

"Ah, you are the gentleman whose coach we are to convey to Wootton Bassett and detach there?" replied Henry.

"Indeed. Now then, Driver, as you are conducting me and my staff, there are certain conditions which I insist upon when being conveyed by train. To begin with, I dislike excessive speed and fifty miles per hour is the maximum I permit. Secondly, I require my saloon to be placed with at least two coaches before and behind mine, for safety's sake. Your inspector tells me he has instructed his staff to attach it to the rear of your train. This is highly unsatisfactory and I will not allow it. You must alter your arrangements. Furthermore, black or even dark smoke from your engine is unacceptable, so you will instruct your fireman accordingly."

Henry could not believe his ears. This little popinjay was effectively telling him how to drive his train! Yet Henry also knew how the Great Western Railway liked politeness in its servants where passengers were concerned. He decided to master his indignation while retaining his adherence to his normal, regulation driving practice.

"I will endeavour, my lord, to attend to your wishes, but I have my own instructions as to how I am to proceed with my driving and these, I fear, may not always comply with your requests."

"I am, Driver, as perhaps I did not make clear to you, a senior official of the Great Western Railway Company and consequently my wishes are to be firmly respected."

"I do apologise, my lord, but we are always informed if we are to convey senior officials and no such information was given this morning. May I ask what exactly your official position is?"

By this time, his lordship was beginning to show his impatience with this impertinent driver, and his tone became more belligerent.

"I must say, Driver, that I find your attitude somewhat disrespectful. I am in fact the owner of a considerable number of shares in the Company and have hence a great deal of influence in the running of its affairs."

"Might I point out, your lordship, that being a shareholder is not an official position in the company."

Lord Willoughby's face turned a dark red with anger but just as he was about to explode, Caleb Herriot, Henry's fireman, muttered, "We've got the starter, Henry."

Henry nodded to him then turned back to Lord Willoughby. "I regret, your lordship, that I cannot debate the issue any longer; we have been given the starter signal to proceed and I am required to follow the guard's instruction. However, if you wish to pursue the matter further, let me assist you by informing you that I am Driver Henry Denton in the top passenger link at Chippenham Shed. You may, of course, make of that information what you will. The guard has already indicated that your coach is safely attached, according to regulations, and as he has also blown his whistle for us to start, I would strongly recommend that your lordship board your saloon immediately."

Henry moved away from the cabside, leaving his lordship spluttering with anger and hurrying back to his coach.

"That's got him off our backs for a while, Caleb," smiled Henry.

"Yes, Henry, well done, but I worry about the consequences if he's as important as he says." Caleb was concerned for the future of his driver. It was well known that important passengers sometimes had the ear of management, to the detriment of staff careers; even when said staff were innocent.

"We might get some support from the platform inspector," commented Henry. "He gave me the impression he was expecting trouble."

"Well, we won't be getting trouble for a while, Henry." Caleb was looking back along the train. "We've got the green!"

On leaving Reading, Henry took his watch out from his waistcoat pocket. "We have to try and catch up twenty minutes before we reach Wootton Bassett," he said. "Shouldn't be too hard if we aren't held up anywhere." Their big 4-2-2 locomotive of the Alma class was almost twenty years old but it was in good condition and running smoothly.

But, to their annoyance, there was a hold-up in Didcot.

"What's the problem, Caleb, can you see?"

The fireman was staring out of the cab down the platform.

"I can see the guard on the platform, Henry, I think he's talking to his lordship."

"Damn the man! Why can't he stop interfering with our train?" Henry was looking angrily at his watch. "We're twenty-two minutes down now."

The whistle was blown and they moved off again. "I'm going to see what the old girl can do now, Caleb, so your shirt is going to get wet!"

"Ready and willing, Henry," replied Caleb with a grin. "Tally ho!" He dug his shovel deeply into the coal in the tender and worked as fast as he could, spreading a dozen shovelfuls across the front of the firebox, allowing the coal to rattle down and giving the fire plenty to bite on.

Within five miles, they were racing along and Henry, counting the mileposts, thought they were doing about seventy miles an hour. They slowed down slightly as they passed through Uffington, with all signals showing clear, and picked up speed once more when they were clear of the points and crossings. They were soon touching seventy again.

"You know, Caleb, when I first took up my duties with the GWR in the early sixties, the narrow gauge trackwork was fairly rough compared to our broad gauge. It took Brunel a while until he got his ideas sorted but, once he had, his track was much smoother. I went north three years back to see my parents and of course by this time the train was narrow gauge from Paddington right through to Chester. I was surprised to find that the new standard gauge track, as we are now told to call it, was as good as our broad gauge. I still prefer the broad gauge because I've got used to it and I'm sad that it is to be abandoned soon. I can see why of course, it's simply no longer practical."

"When do you think it'll go then, Henry?"

"I don't think it will last after Sir Daniel's gone. Gooch is very fond of it but he's well into his sixties."

When they reached Wootton Bassett they had made up almost fifteen minutes and were only seven minutes down. Henry was feeling happier. Like all drivers, he hated being late, even when it was not his fault. There was always a report to be made about late arrivals and if the driver was found to be responsible then a wage deduction could be expected. But Henry's happiness was to be short-lived. There was an altercation on the platform between Lord Willoughby and the Wootton Bassett stationmaster, whose presence had been demanded by his lordship.

Lord Willoughby returned to his coach and the stationmaster walked over to Henry. "I'm sorry, Henry," he said, but we'll have use your engine to detach his lordship's coach; the station pilot has been failed and we've nothing else spare today." Henry muttered something beneath his breath and the stationmaster chuckled. "I know how you feel, but I want you to do me and the yardmaster a favour. Shunt that coach into the long siding, then we'll know where it is quickly as his lordship wants to make an early return tomorrow back to Reading.'

"Yessir."

"Make sure it's well behind the goods shed."

"Behind the goods shed?" Henry was surprised. "That part of the siding hasn't been used for years; nobody will see it there!"

"That's the idea. Some of the young mischief-makers on station staff here won't see it so won't think to fool around with it. You know what some of them are like. Tomorrow morning, we'll know where it is and it will be easy to retrieve when he wants to go back to Paddington."

The crewmen did as they were told but they were now almost thirty minutes down and Caleb was looking worried as they left the station. But Henry started to laugh heartily, as they passed a works train backing into the refuge where they had stabled his lordship's coach. The train carried a team of workmen collecting a range of tools from the vans.

"What's so funny?" Caleb queried.

"Do you know what those workmen are doing?" replied Henry.

"Err – no."

"It's the stationmaster's revenge! That's a re-gauging gang; they'll remove the broad gauge rail from that siding, starting at the points, and won't see Lord Popinjay's coach behind the shed until they've reached the curve. He'll not be getting away quickly tomorrow. He really shouldn't have annoyed our stationmaster!"

"But won't we get into trouble?"

"Not us! The stationmaster will claim he thought we had been informed and will express his deep regret that we hadn't. He won't let us down. Now you'll have to put your back into it; we've got some time to catch up before we reach Bristol."

It was several weeks later that Henry received a notice to attend a meeting at Paddington, to explain his part in a misunderstanding at Wootton Bassett relating to Lord Willoughby's saloon. His lordship's many complaints were read out, with Lord Willoughby listening and smirking. The superintendent carefully noted down all the details on a sheet of paper.

"Now, your lordship, I would be very much obliged if you would kindly sign this for me."

Lord Willoughby beamed. "Why, certainly I will. We must put a stop to these upstart drivers who do not know their proper station in life." He signed with a triumphant flourish.

"Thank you, your lordship," the superintendent said. "You can rest assured that firm and appropriate action will be taken on this matter."

Lord Willoughby nodded briefly, placed his top hat on his head, and marched out in obvious satisfaction. The superintendent folded the signed complaint sheet carefully and dropped it neatly into the wastepaper basket.

"There," he said. "I've taken 'firm and appropriate action'. That man's an infernal nuisance; it would be more in the company's interest to drop *him* in the bin. Thank you, Driver Denton, that will be all."

17 - Driver Denton meets an Iron Duke (November 1891)

There had been talk among shed staff of a powerful new engine coming soon out of Swindon, for the heavier express services to the west. Most of them were designed to run on the standard gauge, although a small number of them were built for the remaining broad gauge main line to Plymouth and Cornwall; this popular route had not yet been converted and was still very busy.

Chief Mechanical Engineer William Dean's new engines were designed with the 2-2-2 wheel arrangement but those few for the broad gauge were built as 'convertibles', because they were designed to be altered to standard gauge running as soon as the broad gauge closed. This was anticipated to be completed in the early summer of 1892.

Driver reports, along with maintenance and coal consumption records, confirmed that the older engines were no longer comfortable handling the heavier loads that were required. Even the rebuilt Iron Duke classes were finding themselves pushed to the limits and were not able to handle the South Devon banks. The final route to Penzance was taken mostly by the ex-Bristol & Exeter tank engines, but they could not always keep the timing that the public had come to expect from the Great Western Railway's route to the ocean terminals at Plymouth, or the holidays beyond, in Cornwall.

One day in early November, Henry was listed to run an express from Bristol to Paddington with fireman Jackie Cornwell. They were to pick up their train at Bristol, taking over from a Newton Abbot crew. When the train appeared dead on time, Henry's eyes widened as he saw that the engine was one of Dean's latest Achilles class locomotives. He had not driven one before but had heard good things about them from other drivers and was looking forward to trying one out. He was told that they could manage the heavier expresses well, keeping good time with them.

The engine came to a stop where he was waiting and he climbed eagerly up into the cab.

"I've never driven one of these. How is she?" he asked the Plymouth driver.

"She's a good 'un," smiled the latter, "Ye'll have no problem with 'er."

Henry was pleased, "Looks like we're in luck, Jackie my lad," he said. "We'll have a good run for a change." Their earlier runs with the rebuilt Iron Duke class had not all been happy. "Nip out and see what her name is," he added while he checked the cab gauges. No difficulty there; most GWR locomotives had very similar cab arrangements by design so that drivers felt at home immediately.

"She's got no name, Mr Denton, only a number," puffed Jackie as he climbed back into the cab and began to check the fire and the gauges.

"No name?" Henry sounded disappointed.

"Just the number: 3028." Jackie did not understand what seemed to have upset his driver.

"Hmm, only the narrow gauge engines have just numbers; must be the trend for the future," Henry said. "A shame, really, I like express engines to have names; it gives them a sort of dignity. How would you like to be known as a number? I'd be calling you 4793."

"I'd hate it!" replied Jackie vehemently. "And our Sally would be 4794! No, it wouldn't do!"

"You've got it, Jackie, it wouldn't do. We had once had class of engines known as Iron Dukes. D'you know why they called one *Wellington*?"

"No."

"The Duke of Wellington was often called the 'Iron Duke', Jackie! Didn't your history teacher tell you about the Battle of Waterloo?"

"Oh, him! He's the fellow who won the battle, wasn't he? England's great hero who defeated Napoleon."

"Well, not quite. Either you weren't listening properly or your teacher was ignorant," said Henry. "He didn't win the battle on his own. The eighty-year-old Prussian General Blücher arrived in the nick of time with his own army. It was a very near-run thing. But never mind your history lesson now, you've got a fire to look after."

Jackie glanced around the cab. "Well, it might be a new engine but it's not very different to others we've been in." He got busy with his shovel while they waited for the guard's green flag. It came within a minute.

"Right," stated Henry, straightening his shoulders. "Let's see what she's made of." He lifted the regulator tentatively and the engine immediately began to move away, smoothly and without any hesitation, with the train. By the time they had stopped in Bath, Henry was beginning to realise that this new engine was a definite improvement on anything he had driven previously, but he was not prepared to confirm his initial thought until they had climbed past the summit of their run and were approaching Swindon.

The first part of the run was exhilarating; the engine seemed to be master of the load and the speed uphill left nothing to be desired. The only problem Henry noticed was a slight jerkiness as they traversed some trackwork that required maintenance. He noted this down in his driver's notebook, for the shedmaster at the engine's home shed. It might be worth looking into by the permanent-way workers.

For both Henry and Jackie, the run from Swindon to Paddington was one of the best they had experienced. The route was, broadly speaking, less hilly; which had been the reason for Brunel picking Swindon as the place to change engines when the GWR was established. In those inaugural days, more powerful engines were needed from Bristol to Swindon than those from Paddington. This also accounted for his choice of the town for the locomotive works, in spite of its lack of suitable water, which had to be piped in from several miles away.

On their arrival in Paddington, the replacement crew were already waiting on the platform and, as Henry and Jackie had, mounted up into the cab to ask about this new type of locomotive, which they had never driven before.

"After we've turned and serviced her, we're taking her back to Bristol on a down express, Henry," explained Ted Throgmorton, the replacement driver, known to one and all as 'Froggy' (his cockney mates found an 'f' easier to handle than the 'th'), "and I wanted to hear from you what she's like."

Henry paused before answering. "You'll have a dream run, Froggy. She's good: in fact, she's very good, but you'll have to steady her a bit on rough patches of track. Watch her when you're belting through that awful pointwork at Reading. In my view, she's a bit unstable at speed. Aside from that, she'll give you every satisfaction."

"Looking forward to the run then. Thanks, Henry."

It was a week later when they met once more, this time exchanging engines in Bristol. Froggy was returning to his Westbourne Park shed at Paddington, on an express goods to Acton.

"How did you like your run on that Dean Single the other day, Froggy?" asked Henry.

"Well, like you said, Henry," replied Henry, "she ran very well and had no problem hauling the express, but you were right about the rough track. I was careful through Reading as you warned me, but I noticed that she could be a little unsteady when running fast. I made a note in the log about that, but I wonder sometimes if anyone ever reads what we write in our logs."

Henry laughed, "One of my mates writes nonsense in his; on a cold day he writes 'warm day', or 'heavy rain' when the sun shines. Nobody's picked him up yet."

"What does he write when there's a serious problem?"

"Oh, he makes sure to tell Shedmaster Melrose about that and checks what he's written in his log correctly."

Froggy nodded a slow agreement, "At least he takes serious matter seriously."

But for Henry the new locomotive was not the only novelty that November. Martha went into labour and produced a son. Little George brought immense happiness to the new parents. Henry and Martha's pride knew no bounds; they adored the little lad and Henry found great delight in listening to his gurgling, and even burping.

Unlike many fathers, he enjoyed holding the child and carrying him about the house; much to his wife's surprise and pleasure, although he drew the line at changing the baby's smalls.

The news about young George had gone round the shed like wildfire and the arrival of the youngest Denton was vigorously celebrated one evening in the local hostelry. Henry went on duty the next morning with a slightly sore head, thankful that he was only on shunting duties that day. He had always been abstemious and after that day's celebration he determined not to sin again.

As the weeks went by, Henry began to notice that more of the trackwork needed attention but was not receiving it. He knew the reason, of course. The company was on the horns of a dilemma: on the one hand, it did not want to spend money on repacking rail joints and reballasting what would soon be removed anyway, but on the other hand it wished to keep its passengers and trains safe.

Henry was rostered several times more on Dean's new Achilles class 2-2-2s, as they became known, and developed an increasing liking for them. Aside from the care needed over less well-aligned track, they seemed to be masters of passenger trains on all but the very hilly routes and had a remarkable turn of speed. They were popular both with the passengers and the company because they were able to keep time well and helped to maintain the Great Western's eminent position with reference to the other major railway companies in the kingdom.

But elsewhere in the country, other railway companies were attracting public attention. The London & North Western, together with the Caledonian, was beginning to compete against the Great Northern in conjunction with the North Eastern and the North British for the fastest run between London and Scotland. This was to culminate in victory for the West Coast line but both groups could see danger inherent in continuing the races, if drivers were encouraged into excessive speeds, and so they agreed to stop them.

The Great Western had its own race: it was more concerned with the London and South Western. Both companies ran to Plymouth, where transatlantic liners were docking, and both were looking for ways to accelerate their runs to London. This actually became a long-standing rivalry, running into the grouping in 1923, and only ceased when the liners began to dock in Southampton rather than Plymouth, effectively giving the Southern Railway victory over the Great Western.

But another matter was occupying Henry's attention. He was interested in whether Martha would be prepared to move to Westbury when the broad gauge was finally closed. They had casually discussed the move already but had not given it detailed consideration. However, rumours were circulating that a new route to the west, from Reading through Westbury to Bristol, was being considered. This would significantly increase the importance of Westbury, as well as reduce the travel time to the West.

"Henry, I think we should have a look again at Westbury, and see about getting a house there before the prices all go up," said Martha one evening as they were preparing for bed. Surprised at her sudden interest and again impressed by her perspicacity, Henry agreed instantly. He hadn't expected her to have heard the railway's rumours.

On his next day off, they visited the town, found a suitable house, and began an exchange of postal correspondence with the owners, who seemed unsure about how much they were prepared to sell for. But Martha and Henry too were in something of a quandary: their proposed move would necessarily rely on Henry's success in transferring to Westbury. The matter of a house price was left in abeyance until Henry's transfer was confirmed.

Their final decision was made over Christmas, when the

Great Western Railway announced that all broad gauge services would cease on the weekend of 22nd May 1892. After that, all the remaining Broad Gauge stock would be stored in Swindon, either to be converted to standard gauge or scrapped.

18 - Driver Denton's broad gauge finale (May 1892)

Henry Denton had been a top-link passenger driver at Chippenham Shed now for ten years now and had earned an enviable reputation as a highly reliable and competent driver. He and Martha had finally made a firm offer on their chosen house in Westbury, not far from the town centre, and were renting in Chippenham until he could organise a transfer. The Westbury shedmaster had assured him there would very soon be a vacancy as one of his senior drivers was experiencing poor eyesight, which would preclude him from driving. The shedmaster had heard of Henry's reputation and was willing to give serious attention to his request for a transfer.

One day in early in May, Driver Denton saw on the enginemen's board at the shed that his duty for the day with Fireman Cornwell was to take an express passenger from Paddington to Newton Abbot on its way to Plymouth. They would travel to Paddington as passengers on a Bristol to Paddington semi-fast.
    Many of these less important trains were already standard gauge. It had been announced some months previously that all broad gauge trains would finally cease running towards the end of the month, so Henry assumed this might well be his last main run on the broad gauge. He had been a dedicated broad gauge man since his transfer to Oxford at the age of twenty. He was now forty-four. He had, of course, frequently driven standard gauge trains and was familiar with the smaller cabs of those locomotives. He had once felt much more at home firing and driving on broad gauge locomotives but in recent years this feeling had become less important. Furthermore, broad gauge track maintenance had necessarily become a lower priority, which made driving on it less of the pleasure it had

once been. But he also realised, with some regret, that his little son George would never have the thrill of riding on a broad gauge train with his father at the regulator.

"Ready for your last run on the proper railway, Henry?" Platform Inspector Harrison was waiting at the end of the platform at Paddington when Henry reached the waiting locomotive. He observed that it was another of the Dean Singles, with which he had hauled a Paddington express a few months earlier.

"Yes sir," he nodded, "and I wish it wasn't. I liked Brunel's vision right from the first time I came across it in Wolverhampton many years ago when I was still a younker."

"I agree," replied the inspector, "I think the Gauge Commissioners erred when they decided in favour of Stephenson's gauge for the whole country. We missed a great opportunity then."

"I suppose we did," replied Henry, "but I can understand their final choice. I believe that the country then had well over a thousand miles of narrow gauge against the 200 miles of broad gauge of the Great Western and its associates. Back then, there was the cost of changing to the broad gauge for all the other bickering companies."

The inspector nodded. "Yes, Henry, you're quite right of course, but you have to credit Brunel for his determination to continue; he stuck to his guns and belief that his gauge was superior."

"Oh, I entirely agree, sir. I am certain that if we had accepted his broad gauge across the country, we would now have a railway capable of carrying far more passengers and freight than is possible today. He should have been consulted before Stephenson!"

The inspector smiled. "Yes indeed, but not as a locomotive engineer! His engine designs were almost useless. He was lucky enough to have Daniel Gooch build our engines for him!"

Meanwhile in the cab, Jackie was chatting to the servicing crew, who had brought the polished and gleaming engine from the cleaners at Westbourne Park Shed. As the crew departed, Henry touched his cap to the inspector and climbed up.

"Well, Jackie, let's see what we have here."

It was a real pleasure to find a cab that was not just clean but also brand new. He glanced down the platform at the crowd of passengers. There were more than usual because it was widely announced that the broad gauge was closing soon and many wanted a final ride on what they considered to be one of the best railway trips in the kingdom.

Henry's first impression, gained from his earlier run on a Dean Single, was reinforced as they left Paddington. The big engine easily had the measure of its heavy train and they were soon speeding through London's western suburbs, with its factories situated alongside the line especially for the convenient railway access. They pulled into Reading dead on time, with Jackie having been able to put his shovel down more often than with older locomotives, for several minutes at a time, to stretch his shoulders and arms and release the tension.

"Easy to fire as well, Mr Denton," he said. "Always provided you don't want to get me shovelling my arms off somewhere before Taunton?"

"You can rest easy on that score, Jackie," replied Henry. "Unless, of course, we hit trouble somewhere. Then I might have to take the shovel for a while if your arms threaten to drop off." This last remark was made with a sense of mischief. Jackie was the most efficient fireman that Henry had ever had in the cab, and they both knew it.

Their Dean Single was not the one they had taken earlier but there was no appreciable difference that they could detect as a result of Dean's standardisation of cab layout. These engines were the most capable locomotives they had ever had for the heavily loaded West of England trains. Nevertheless, Henry took care driving over stretches of track which he knew from experience to be rough, and he remembered the track through Reading. Here, he took care, but even so the engine ran through the station without the smoothness that he would have hoped for, and he noted this in his engineman's notebook. Apart from his concern regarding smooth running, he enjoyed the strength and power that these engines made available to him.

The next fortnight, he spent on standard gauge (he had now got used to the term) trains, in a range of duties, but another matter arose, taking his mind off day-to-day work matters. He received a letter from the Westbury shedmaster, stating that the expected driving vacancy had cropped up and asking if Henry would like to come for an interview. Henry decided that, now the broad gauge work had virtually ceased for him and he could expect no more big engine duties, he could apply and possibly make the move.

The interview was successful and he was even able to persuade Jackie Cornwell to come with him, filling one of three other vacancies at Westbury Shed.

Henry and Martha took the opportunity to visit the owners of the house they liked, who had finally agreed on a price of £145, and made preparations to move in.

"We're going to have to pull our belts in for a while, my love," said Henry to Martha as he set out to the bank to arrange payment for the move. His wife just smiled. He was back shortly with a statement and a startled expression on his face.

"I can't understand it," he said. "We've got nearly thirty pounds more than I expected!"

"I am so glad you leave money matters to me, my love," she replied. "Your allowance for housekeeping has permitted me to put a little aside each week for several years now!"

Henry stared at her. "I always knew that marrying you was a sound move, but I wasn't entirely sure why! Now," he continued, "while little George is sound asleep, I need you upstairs for fifteen minutes!"

He led her to the staircase to their bedroom.

"Is fifteen minutes all I'm getting?" she murmured plaintively. "Hardly even time to get undressed."

Henry's move from Chippenham Shed was celebrated in style. He had been a popular and well-respected colleague and they were sad to lose him. Jackie took part in the festivity as well, although he had two weeks more to work before his own move to Westbury. Their work consisted entirely of standard gauge duties because the broad gauge track had already been lifted. Whenever they worked north to Swindon, however, Jackie noticed that Henry still gazed longingly at the remaining temporary broad gauge sidings that had been laid to hold the huge amount of stock stored before it could be either converted or scrapped.

Many of the enginemen that Henry and Jackie now worked with had never been on broad gauge locomotives and couldn't really understand the attraction to them. The ex-broad gauge men, however, generally felt as Henry did, and had always believed in the inherent superiority of Brunel's gauge, regretting its demise.

One morning, the shedmaster called Henry into his office with a written request from Swindon for him and Fireman Cornwell to work there 'on special duties' for a fortnight.

"What's that all about, Henry?" asked Jackie.

"I have no idea. The letter didn't specify what our duties were to be."

A very puzzled crew took an early train north to find out what they were required for. It was quite strange to see that virtually all the mixed gauge track around Swindon had been removed and was now completely standard gauge. They were directed to report to an officer in the staffing office.

"You men have been picked out because you have been an effective team," said the officer in the Swindon office. "The track you will be working on has been poorly laid and it needs special care. We don't want more derailments than necessary." Poorly laid track? Both men couldn't believe their ears. Why would the GWR – if it was the GWR – lay poor track anywhere? It didn't make sense.

"Ah!" said Henry, as the penny dropped. "The broad gauge storage sidings!"

"Exactly," agreed the officer. "I know it's not what you're used to but it has to be done, and as quickly as possible. We need the space and to clear the old stock to achieve this. We hope to be able to have scrapped or converted most of it by the end of the year. We are choosing a number of experienced crews each fortnight to complete the job."

For two weeks, Henry and Jackie shunted stock either to the works for conversion to standard gauge, or to the designated scrapyard sidings where vehicles were stripped of what could still be used, such as wheels, couplings and cab fittings. The work was undoubtedly boring, but at least they were given one of the old South Devon Railway's 4-4-0ST tank engines, *Leopard,* for the job, which made it easy. Some of these old engines still had plenty of life in them. Henry and Jackie felt instantly at home but it was sad to know that these engines too were due for the scrapyard when they had finished their work.

While they were shunting some coaches into the conversion sidings on their last morning on this duty, Jackie commented, "Who was it said that something was 'from the sublime to the ridiculous'? I heard it was Napoleon. That fits our job rather well."

Henry shook his head dejectedly. "There is a much earlier and far more appropriate statement about what we are doing, Jackie," he replied, staring sadly at a long line of the old Iron Dukes rusting away on an adjacent siding: "'How are the mighty fallen!'"

19 – Henry's conquest at Wellington (November 1903)

It was now eleven years since the final closure and dismantling of the broad gauge, and Henry had got used to working entirely with standard gauge rolling stock. He still felt a yearning from time to time for the roomy cabs and previous smoother running of the huge engines of the old gauge, in contrast to the early, and relatively rough, standard gauge tracks of the previous century. Across the country, standards in most railway companies had improved to such an extent that really poor trackwork was only to be found on little-used branches and sidings. Henry was also finding that the newer engines designed for the GWR by Mr Churchward, once Mr Dean's assistant, were proving to be a spectacular advancement in power over even the latest of Mr Dean's engines. It was believed by many in the company that Churchward had had a hand in Dean's designs well before the latter retired.

Mr Dean seemed to have shown signs of mental fatigue in his final years at the helm and had allowed his assistant to try out some of his own design ideas.

Henry had driven Dean's 4-4-0 Atbara class locomotives on occasions, and found them good, strong engines on express passenger services. He had heard of a new variant, the City class, which were basically the same but with Churchward's tapered boilers instead of the parallel boilers of the Atbaras.

He was waiting at Plymouth Millbay Station to take over an express passenger for Paddington, as far as Swindon. From there, they could return to their shed at Westbury, where he and his regular fireman Jimmy Henshaw would come off duty.

He and Jimmy had been working together for several years now, since Jackie Cornwell had been promoted to

Driver, and they were very comfortable with each other.

They were sitting on a bench as their coaches were slowly backing in, propelled by the train engine, which they assumed would be an Atbara.

"I hope those loco servicing fellows have done their job, Mr Denton, and broken up the coal nicely," remarked Jimmy. "We've had a heavy day already and I don't want to have to break my back on the way home."

"Don't worry about it," replied Henry. "The South Devon banks'll keep you busy but just think about that easy run down Wellington Bank, south-west of Taunton. If you prepare the fire well, you can sit back on your arse and enjoy the ride!"

At that moment, they both saw a clerical gentleman with a smile on his face, striding towards them.

"Morning, Reverend!" Henry greeted him. "Have you met my fireman, Jimmy Henshaw?"

"Good morning, Driver Denton. And good morning to you too, Fireman Henshaw."

Henry turned to Jimmy: "Jimmy, Reverend Beesley is one of those gentlemen who give us railwaymen great pleasure. He checks our speed and lets us know how we are doing – writes up logs of our journeys, as he calls them."

"How do you do that, Reverend Beesley?" enquired Jimmy.

"Oh, it's not hard; we just count the telegraph poles as we pass them and check the time on a stopwatch. The poles are usually a set distance apart and we use that measurement to calculate the time and hence the speed. We also get details of the train load and engines, including coal and water consumed."

The train had pulled up and the reverend turned to look for a compartment. "I'll be getting out in Bristol, Henry," he said, "and we'll have a quick chat then."

"Very good of—" Henry began and then stopped and stared at the train engine. He had assumed it would be an Atbara, but this had a larger, higher-pitched, tapered boiler.

"Goodness me, Jimmy," he exclaimed, "they've given us a City today!"

"So they have!" As the engine approached, Henry caught sight of its name, *City of Chester*.

"Well look at that!" Henry rubbed his hands with pleasure. "My home town! Let's see what she can do; I've never driven one of these!"

"My poor back!" muttered Jimmy as he opened the firebox doors to check the fire. He knew very well what Henry's enthusiasm promised. Reverend Beesley smiled; he too knew how Henry enjoyed fast driving. "I'll be sure to let you have the full details of your run," he said as he left.

The first tough run was out of Plymouth and as far as Brent, and their City class 4-4-0 seemed to manage its train with a degree of ease not often seen with an Atbara. Jimmy was relieved because modifications did not always fulfil their promised improvement. It was, however, on the downhill run to Newton Abbot that both crewmen were to find that this engine had something different. It ran much more easily with their train than they would expect. Jimmy began to worry about the next stage of their trip, over the moors. Although he knew he would have to shovel hard again until Newton Abbot, he wondered what his driver was planning for the stretch between Wellington and Taunton. This contained the well-known Wellington Bank, where many drivers liked to open up on the long downhill run, claiming they had to make up time but in reality using this excuse for the enjoyment of seeing their engines run. This was especially true when they had an engine in good nick.

Jimmy knew he was a competent fireman and that Henry trusted him, which only increased his apprehension when he noticed Henry glance into the firebox while they stopped at Tiverton Junction for a signal check. He recalled nervously what the reverend gentleman had said about timing their train and saw that Henry had a grin on his face. They had been held up for several minutes at the junction and Driver Denton, uncharacteristically, had not shown any impatience at all. Normally, he would have been peering about to see what the hold-up was, muttering about the slackness of incompetent signal bobbies.

"Jimmy, my lad," said Henry as they moved off, "we're going to see what she's made of."

Jimmy's concern was justified: they were going to run! He hoped Henry would remember that a train arriving ahead of time could generate awkward questions for the crew, and that platform inspectors at Taunton were well aware of the temptations for drivers down the bank. Jimmy realised why his driver had not shown impatience at Tiverton Junction; Henry had wanted to be delayed to give him a reason for speeding down Wellington Bank!

There was a further problem: the train was an Ocean Mails special and had only five coaches; this was a train that even one of Dean's Singles could manage at speed. Jimmy could remember many fast runs with Driver Denton at the regulator racing a Single, and keeping his fireman busy. Jimmy could not understand how Henry managed to keep out of platform inspectors' clutches; he always seemed to know how to stay within limits.

"Now then, Fireman Cornwell," began Henry, well before they had reached Wellington Bank, "it's time you did a spot of driving again."

Henry, like most drivers, had often handed the regulator over to his fireman to give him practice at driving. This was only done with firemen who could be trusted, of course.

"Something else as well," he continued. "We've been a good team for long enough now for you to call me Henry."

Jimmy knew this was a confidence booster. It worked.

"Thank you, Mr – er – Henry," replied Jimmy, "I really appreciate that!" He took hold of the regulator to familiarise himself with its feel of this new engine.

"You've got about ten minutes before the bank. I'll take over when we're heading down it."

Jimmy nodded, looking ahead out of the cab while keeping hold of the big lever. Henry carefully shovelled more coal just to trim the fire and glanced at the water gauges to his own satisfaction, in readiness for their downhill run.

"I'll take over now, Jimmy," Henry said as they reached the top of the bank and Jimmy reluctantly handed over. He picked up the shovel, ready for any firing needed, although a quick glance into the firebox showed that none would be required for a while. Clearly, Henry had not forgotten how to fire. Jimmy tried to recall what the clergyman had said about counting the telegraph poles as they sped downhill. He had time to relax during the following quarter-hour or so; something always appreciated by firemen. However, he remained rather tense as he watched the mileposts flying by. There was no dial recording their speed in the cab, but he knew from experience that they were flying.

As they reached the bottom of the bank, Henry took out his watch, frowned and lowered the regulator. They were slowing down, but Jimmy saw the face of an official as they raced through Taunton; his eyebrows were raised and Jimmy saw how he also took out his watch. Jimmy didn't like to think how fast they must have been travelling.

At Temple Meads Station in Bristol, while they were waiting for the starter signal, Reverend Beesley came up to the cab once more. He had a serious expression on his face.

"I don't think I should tell you what your speed was down the bank, Henry. I am uncertain whether the public or even the Great Western Railway is ready to hear what you just did!"

"What was it, do you think?"

Reverend Beesley avoided an answer, at first asking, "Did you slow the train down near the foot of the bank at all?"

"Yes, very slightly. I thought we might have been going too fast."

"I had a minor problem with my stopwatch, so I cannot be certain, but I recorded a speed of just over ninety-six miles an hour at the fastest point."

The reverend lifted his hat as he departed, just as a platform inspector came over to the cab. He had a grin on his face as he addressed Henry.

"Bit tempted were we, Driver Denton? I know you drivers like to run down that bank, but you nearly overdid it today. You came in three minutes early. Another two minutes and you would have faced a severe reprimand and a fine. You're lucky I didn't believe the report an inspector at

Taunton telegraphed through to me."

"Thank you, sir," said Henry. "I haven't driven one of these new City class engines before and wasn't quite sure how she would run," he explained.

"Yes," agreed the inspector as he turned to hide the grin on his face, "and my dog has five legs! Just watch yourself, Henry!"

The starter signal dropped and Henry took his train gently out of Bristol, towards the east and Paddington.

"We got a bit lucky there, Jimmy," he muttered as they were approaching Bath. "We'd better keep our mouths shut about that run down the bank. I suspect we might have cracked the hundred and Rev. Beesley didn't want to tell us. These engines are capable of it."

"Yes, but I'm glad we don't know for sure, if it comes to that," said Jimmy. "I can think of several drivers who would want to have a go, and what's more," he added ruefully, "I can think of many poor bloody firemen who've have to do the hard work to get up the bank first!"

"Mmm," said Henry, ignoring Jimmy's comment, "I wonder when someone will do it."

"And what'll happen to him when he does," added Jimmy.

He didn't have to wonder long. It happened the following year and the crew concerned were threatened with instant dismissal if they breathed a word about it. In fact, the GWR did not publicly admit the speed for almost twenty years.

20 - A Star is born (September 1907)

It had been some four years since Henry's exhilarating run down Wellington Bank near Taunton with a City class 4-4-0 and he had had several similar runs with other locomotives since then, including one fascinating run driving one of the French imports. The Chief Mechanical Engineer, George Churchward, had persuaded the company to purchase three of the renowned 4-4-2 locomotives, which were achieving such impressive results in France. He wanted to see what he could learn from them and whether there was anything worth copying. Churchward had built a new design of 4-6-0 engines for the express passenger services but some were converted to 4-4-2s for comparison purposes. They were named after ladies in Sir Walter Scott's stories, and other fictional females.

Henry too had been deeply impressed by the speed and power of the French engines, which had shown distinct superiority over the Cities. Truth be told, the smaller 4-4-0 Cities, fine engines though they undoubtedly were, were finding the heavier West of England expresses rather more than they could easily handle. Churchward was looking for a long-term replacement class of engines that could handle the heavier passenger trains the traffic department was anticipating.

"We'll be busy today, Jimmy," said Henry one morning as they booked on at Westbury Shed. "We have a local freight to Bristol, an express passenger to Paddington, and then returning home on another!" Their engine for the local freight was one of the older Armstrong 2-4-0 general purpose engines, but it was well past its best days and, in Henry's opinion, a very poor performer. It wheezed and clanked its leisurely way, making timekeeping rather difficult, until they finally brought it into the yard at

Bristol, where they thankfully delivered it into the hands of the replacement crew.

"What's she like, then?" asked the new driver, climbing aboard.

"If you want my honest opinion, she's ready for the scrapyard," replied Henry, grimly. "You'll save yourself trouble if you take her there directly."

"Bad as that, huh?"

Henry nodded and left to walk with Jimmy to Temple Meads Station, where they were to pick up their express. Both men were a little depressed after a disappointing run and were hoping for something better on the up Paddington.

It came in right on time and the engine crew welcomed them into the cab with smiles. Things were beginning to look up.

"You'll enjoy your run on this engine, Henry," said the driver, "Swindon's new 4-6-0s are fine engines. Furthermore," he grinned, "This one will tickle your fancy especially: she's called *Lady Godiva*!"

Jimmy heard this and chuckled. "We should hand her over to the LNWR," he said. "They should shed her in Coventry."

"You've certainly cheered us up, Jem," replied Henry. "We've just come from a bad run on an old Armstrong 2-4-0. Poor old girl is ready for the scrapyard."

"Well, this 'un'll impress you," said Jem as he and his fireman climbed down to the platform and walked away.

Jem was dead right, thought Henry after they had received the starter signal and moved off out of the station on their way east. The train was a heavy one but he felt quickly that this new engine was master of the load and had no trouble at all in vigorously starting and hauling the dozen coaches at speed. By the time they had reached Swindon, both Henry and Jimmy were delighted. *Lady Godiva* was a thoroughbred. The run from then on, via Didcot and Reading to Paddington, was unadulterated pleasure. Their Lady provided all the speed and power needed; she was very free steaming and light on coal consumption, making Jimmy's job very easy. The only concern was a slow down due to adverse signals passing Slough.

It was almost with regret that they relinquished the controls in the cab in Paddington, to allow a new crew to take the engine back to Old Oak Common Shed for turning and servicing, ready for another run the next day. Henry and Jimmy animatedly informed the new crew about their run from Bristol and the capability of this new locomotive.

They were due to spend the night at a private home near the shed. The landlady there often put up enginemen overnight, before their return to their home shed. As the two men climbed the stairs to the bedroom they were to share, they glimpsed a female figure silently flitting along the landing to the bathroom.

"Did you see who that was? Was it the daughter of the family?" whispered Henry.

"Probably," muttered Jimmy, adding wistfully, "but I wish it had been Lady Godiva."

"It's high time you got married, young Cornwell," returned Henry with mock severity. "You're getting lecherous."

"Oh," said Jimmy innocently, "does marriage cure lechery?"

By this time, they had reached their bedroom and Henry chuckled as they closed the door behind them. "Get married, Jimmy, and you'll find out."

At their early breakfast the following morning, they were served by the young daughter of the landlady, who told them her name was Rosie and she hoped she hadn't disturbed them the previous night. She had been making their bed, she explained, but they had arrived more promptly than she had expected.

On their way to book on at Old Oak Common, Jimmy remarked, "I wish she had stayed in the bedroom. I'd rather have her next to me in bed than you, Henry!"

"Definitely time you got married, Jimmy, you cheeky devil!" laughed Henry. "You'll have to be more diligent to see what's available in Westbury!"

They booked on to find that they were to take another express passenger to Westbury, where Weymouth men would take it over for the rest of the run to the port to link with the Channel Islands ferry.

Their run to the station was with the crew of a little 0-6-0T tank engine whose duty consisted of taking empty coaching stock to and from the terminus. Their train was already at the platform, waiting for the engine to back down from the shed. A platform inspector was waiting there as well.

"We'll be interested in your opinion of this engine, Driver Denton," he said.

"Why's that, sir?" asked Henry.

"You've got another Lady; but this time she's a 4-4-2. Mr Churchward's interested in drivers' opinions as to which wheel arrangement will serve us better."

"I'll keep careful note, sir."

Their Lady backed down a few moments later and Jimmy descended onto the track to couple her up to her train, while Henry checked the cab gauges.

The run out of Paddington confirmed their opinions of this new variation of the engines. These were what enginemen had been waiting for! There was little doubt that they could handle the increased length and weight of trains that the Great Western was hoping for.

For much of their journey to Westbury, they found little difference between the 4-4-2 and the 4-6-0 type of engine, although possibly the latter had the slightest edge on the former. To be certain, Henry thought, it needed a lot more driving. Again, both men almost regretted handing over their charge, to the Weymouth men at Westbury.

Their runs with the two Ladies and the opinions about the differences were, however, forgotten some months later. They were booked to take over a London-bound express at Swindon and when their train entered the station they were surprised to find another new 4-6-0; this was different in that it had, instead of the expected large cylinders on the side, two slightly smaller ones, and another two housed under the smokebox.

"What have we got here, Ted?" Henry asked Driver Henderson as he climbed into the cab to take over the reins. "A four-cylinder Lady?"

His colleague smiled, "No, Henry. This is a Star class engine, and she's brand new. You're in luck!"

"What's lucky about her?"

"Ah, that'd be telling! You'll have to find out for yourselves!" With that, Driver Henderson and his fireman left the cab, chuckling.

"Looks like we're getting no advice on this one, Jimmy," said Henry as they took over and made ready to start their train.

"We'll find out soon enough, I imagine, Henry," replied Jimmy as he checked the fire and aimed three or four shovelfuls of coal where he thought it was a little thin.

For the first dozen or so miles out of Swindon, they could not see what it was Driver Henderson and his mate had been smiling about. Their Star seemed to be doing much the same work as the Ladies they had become familiar with. But shortly before Didcot they ran into a lengthy signal check and had to crawl slowly to the station, where they were delayed for another ten minutes on account of a loading problem on the platform. As a result, they were fifteen minutes down leaving Didcot.

"We're going to have to push her hard, Jimmy, if we're to make up any time between here and Paddington," Henry said grimly. "New engine or not, she's going to have to show her paces!"

They had fourteen well-loaded coaches on leaving Swindon, which meant that the train was a heavy one, but over the relatively short run to Reading they had made up five of the missing fifteen minutes and the engine showed no sign of a struggle with its load. From Reading, Henry opened up the regulator as much as he dared, bearing in mind this was a new engine for him. They were very soon racing at high speed towards the capital.

Jimmy kept the fire in perfect condition and in a short break from firing he looked out of the cab and counted the passing telegraph poles. He leaned over to Henry and over the noise in the cab shouted, "We're doing over eighty, Henry!" He put his back into shovelling once more. But, eighty or not, the cab ride was even steadier at speed than the Ladies.

Cabs were never smooth at any speed in a steam locomotive; both men knew that of course, and this locomotive's splendid performance was something neither had expected. They were still hurtling through Westbourne Park at over seventy before Henry began to reduce their speed and slow the train down to enter the great arches of Paddington exactly on time.

"What a magnificent run, Henry!" exulted Jimmy as they pulled up at the buffers.

Henry nodded his head. "I thought the Ladies were very fine engines, Jimmy, but the Stars are something else again! Four cylinders instead of two gives them the edge over anything else we've got when it comes to power, speed and steady riding."

He paused and pondered for a moment or two while Jimmy busied himself sweeping the cab floor and checking that they had enough of a fire to back into Old Oak Common Shed for servicing.

"I cannot seriously imagine any engine better than this one for the West of England expresses," Henry said slowly. "I believe with these Stars we have one of the finest engines in the whole country, with the Ladies a close second."

"I agree," said Jimmy. "And what's more, I think she could run back to Swindon immediately once she's been serviced and turned."

There was no doubt that Churchward's engines were just as powerful and economical as the more complicated French compound engines he had imported for comparison. Nevertheless, de Glehn's French engines had given him the stimulus for the Ladies and the Stars.

"Just think too, Jimmy," Henry remarked wistfully, "if we'd have stuck to our guns, what Mr Churchward could have accomplished with a Star, built to broad gauge dimensions!

Glossary Of technical railway terms

Banking engine: An engine at the rear of a train assisting by pushing from behind.

Bobby: railway signalmen. The name derives from Sir Robert Peel's police force. It was also used to refer to railway police. (see also 'Peeler')

Brake van: small van at the end of a goods train from which the guard could apply a brake to assist the driver when slowing the train. In a passenger train, the brake van would be a coach with a section for the guard.

Brighton Line: Railwaymen's term for the London, Brighton & South Coast Railway.

Broad gauge: Brunel's original seven foot (and a quarter of an inch) railway gauge for the Great Western Railway, finally abandoned in 1892.

'Coal miners' friend': a term used to describe a driver who was unnecessarily profligate with coal.

Converter wagon: This was a wagon inserted into a short-distance goods train in which vehicles of both gauges could be incorporated. It was built with extra wide buffers in order to accommodate the different distances between broad and standard gauge wagons.

Distant: a signal warning drivers about the status of the section following the one they were entering. (see also 'home' and 'starter')

Driver: the man who controls the locomotive.

Down: the direction from London. (see also **'Up'**)

Dual gauge: Track with three rails to allow both broad and standard gauge trains to use. (see also **'Mixed' gauge**)

Express: A fast train with only limited stops.

Fireman: the man who ensures that the locomotive has sufficient energy for the driver to do his job. Earlier commentaries refer to the fireman as a 'stoker'.

Grouping: The Railways act of 1921 grouped the 120 railway companies into four main groups: the Great Western Railway, the London Midland and Scottish Railway, the London & North Eastern Railway and the Southern Railway.

Guard: the official in charge of a train; he was normally at the rear of the train.

Home: a signal indicating whether the next section is clear. (see also **'distant'** and **'starter'**)

Horsebox: a van specially fitted out for transporting horses

Light engine: an engine travelling without a train.

Mixed gauge: A stretch of broad gauge track within which a third, standard gauge rail has been added to allow trains of both gauges to run. (see also **Dual gauge**)

Motion: the set of coupling and connecting rods linking the driving wheels and the cylinders.

Narrow gauge: Broad gauge enginemen of the GWR referred to the standard gauge as 'narrow.'

'On the cushions': Enginemen returning from duty and not required to drive a locomotive were permitted to travel in comfort with passengers.

'Peeler': A common, early nickname for civilian (i.e. non-railway) police, based on the name of Sir Robert Peel who instituted the original force.

Permanent Way: This is the track and the its foundation which need regular checking.

Pilot engine: engine which would be coupled in front of a train engine and used to assist with a heavy train.

Salop: railway term for Shrewsbury, based on the original Latin.

Semi-fast: a train which does not stop at all stations.

Single: a locomotive with one large driving wheel on each side.

Shunting: a process whereby railway vehicles were moved about to re-arrange trains. It took place in shunting yards and was done either with a locomotive or by using horses and ropes.

Starter: a signal (usually at the end of a platform) to indicate whether a train may move off to the next signal. (see also **'home'** and **'distant'**)

Stoker: see 'fireman'.

Stopper: a train which calls at all stations on its run.

Turntable: a large, revolving table in an engine shed. It permits engines to be turned round.

Up: the direction to London. (See also 'down')

www.ingramcontent.com/pod-product-compliance
Lightning Source LLC
Chambersburg PA
CBHW021153080526
44588CB00008B/319